Straight

from

the Fridge,

_____ Dad

Max Décharné

BROADWAY BOOKS

 NEW YORK

Straight

from

the Fridge,

Dad

a

Dictionary

of

Hipster

Slang

Broadway Books titles may be purchased for business or promotional use or for
special sales. For information, please write to: Special Markets Department,
Random House, Inc., 1540 Broadway, New York, NY 10036.

BROADWAY BOOKS and its logo, a letter B bisected on the diagonal,
are trademarks of Broadway Books, a division of Random House, Inc.

Visit our website at www.broadwaybooks.com.

First Broadway Books trade paperback edition published 2001.

DESIGNED BY TERRY KARYDES

Library of Congress Cataloging-in-Publication Data
Décharné, Max.
Straight from the fridge, dad: a dictionary of hipster slang / Max Décharné.
p. cm.
Originally published: Harpenden, England : No Exit Press, 2000.
1. English language—United States—Slang—Dictionaries.
2. Beat generation—Language—Dictionaries.
3. Hippies—Language—Dictionaries. 4. Americanisms—Dictionaries. I. Title.

PE3727.B43 D43 2001
427'.793'03—dc21   2001035043

ISBN 0-7679-0840-6

1   2   3   4   5   6   7   8   9   10

Für Katja

———————————————

direkt

aus

dem

Kuhlschrank

Acknowledgments

To Ion Mills for saying yes to the book proposal in the first place; to Derek Duerden, Margaret Duerden, Geoffrey Openshaw, Ann Scanlon, and Cathi Unsworth for help and inspiration; and to Ant Hanlon and Stewart Pannaman for all the solid sounds down through the years.

To Gerald Howard for giving the righteous jive a chance to pad some skulls in Uncle Sam's crashpad, and to Jay Crosby, Brian Jones, Betsy Areddy, Catherine Pollock, and everyone at Broadway Books for making it happen.

Thanks also to John Whitfield, Claire Munro, and Sophie Braham for letting me clutter up their office at a time of no sleep and not enough beer.

A very special thank you to Mark Rubenstein of New York (a prime source of the hep, the gone, and the downright wig-tightening), and to Nicole Hofmann, Joe Gardiner, Zoe, and Mr. Wax who passed the good word along.

Most of all, thanks to Katja Klier, for photography, living space, food, and encouragement, without whom this book just couldn't have been written.

Introduction

"Where in English we are concerned with communicating *exactly* what we want to convey and nothing else, the hipster is satisfied if what he says manages to *include* what he means. Imagine the difference between shooting at a dime from twenty paces with a .22 rifle, and with a 40-gauge shotgun, and you will have a rough approximation of the difference between English and Hip."

From the album *How to Speak Hip,*
Del Close and John Brent c. 1961

Back in the old days before the dawn of color TV, genuine hepcats like Cab Calloway and Lavada Durst published dictionaries of hipster slang that took a narrower definition than the present volume and, not surprisingly, wound up with booklets that ran for about twelve pages, although the prize award in this department must go to Babs Gonzales, whose *Boptionary* contains a whole fifty-three phrases spread out over two small, but immaculately cool pages. What you have here is something more inclusive, drawing on phrases and words from pulp novels, classic noir and exploitation films, blues, country, and rock 'n' roll lyrics, and other related sources. Millions of people down through the years have happily read the novels of Raymond Chandler without necessarily knowing exactly what a roscoe might be, and generations of Louis Armstrong fans have enjoyed listening to "Struttin' with Some Barbecue," only occasionally wondering why the great man felt the need to walk around apparently clutching an item of alfresco cooking equipment. If you attempt to use more than a few of these phrases in normal conversation, you'll most likely be shunned by ordinary, decent people or taken away for special tests at a secure establishment in the country somewhere. Nevertheless, even though many of the words in this dictionary may be the product of sick-minded individuals inventing hip phrases to fill out the dialogue in numerous low-budget teen films and crime stories, they have a life of their own, and most of them refuse to lie down and play dead.

Half the people trying to write the "Great American Novel" fifty years ago seemed to think that the best way to do that was to employ an over-educated style which would have made Marcel Proust look like someone with a limited vocabulary, whereas no-nonsense pulp products like *Hot Dames on Cold Slabs* by Michael Storme or *Two Timing Tart* by John Davidson had an entirely different audience in mind. Although the works of great writers like Chandler and Hammett are rich in authentic slang, it's also true that some of the tackiest or most obscure pulp hacks provide the best and most individual examples of hip as it should be spoken. The blues and rockabilly performers of the 1950s were often making records for small labels with only a very limited, local audience, so they could get away with using phrases which might mean something to a farming community in Texas but be completely incomprehensible in New York, such as Hank Stanford's version of "She's a Hum Dum Dinger (from Dingersville)" which contains the immortal line "She's long, she's tall, she's a handsome queen / She's got ways like a mowing machine."

Many of the books and much of the music quoted here, now hailed as classics, were sneered at and marginalized as throwaway entertainment for the lower orders, and were often being produced by people who didn't know if their career was going to last out the week. The general law in such cases seems to be that if you work for peanuts, starve most of the time, and die in almost total obscurity, you are then free to be hailed as a genius. When Jim Thompson died in 1977, none of his books were in print in the United States. Nelson Algren was in a pretty much similar position a few years later at the time of his death, and, by pulp standards, they were two of the howling great success stories. Hell, even Hollywood came calling at relatively regular intervals. Both writers have now been the subject of extensive republication, but, on balance, they probably don't care much one way or the other these days.

In general, the language contained here originated either with jazz musicians or gangsters in the early part of the twentieth century. There's an enormous amount of crossover between these basic reference points, which isn't surprising, since musicians frequently played in venues run by mobsters, and the tough guys with the machine guns were often fans of the music. The well-known tale of Frank Sinatra arriving in Cuba to visit Lucky Luciano and the heads of all the U.S. mafia families in 1947, allegedly carrying a suitcase containing a million green pictures of George Washington, is just one example. Both of these sections of the community enjoyed going to the movies, so once Hollywood started putting out crime films featuring people like Cagney and Bogart, the language was passed around even more, with many real-life hoods trying to dress and behave like George Raft.

It probably won't escape the notice of the more attentive reader that many of these slang phrases concern drink, drugs, sex, and violent crime. Jazz music emerged from the Storyville district of New Orleans, a red-light area so wide open that the government sent in troops in 1917 to close the whole place down, and a life spent hanging round in whorehouses and bargain-basement gambling joints is hardly likely to produce a group of people given to speaking like characters from a Jane Austen novel. Attitudes to women, in particular, sometimes make the average caveman look like a bleeding-heart liberal, but, on the other hand, some of the female characters who show up in film noir and hard-boiled crime fiction are sharp as a razor and nobody's fool. The women portrayed by Veronica Lake, Gene Tierney, Lauren Bacall, and any number of Jim Thompson characters could talk back with the best of them and eat most men for breakfast. Sure, attitudes have changed a lot since those days, but that's true across all sections of society and popular culture—the casual racism of children's comics back in the 1940s, for instance, is breathtaking to modern sensibilities.

The overall tone of hipster slang is a kind of deadpan cynicism—not entirely unexpected from a section of society that often spent much of its time trying to avoid the law and scrape the rent money together. The dark tone and worldview of film noir is all the more understandable when one considers that a great many people responsible for the genre had escaped from Europe one step ahead of Uncle Adolf and his playmates. Flouting some aspects of the law didn't seem particularly strange back in the twenties, once the stern moralists with the big sticks had succeeded in having booze outlawed—a particularly smart move which drove nearly the whole adult population into some sort of contact with organized crime in their search for dishonest refreshment.

The earliest examples of slang given here are from around the turn of the last century, and the most recent are taken from the middle years of the 1960s, which was roughly the time when the people who thought they were cool stopped wearing suits, gave up holding onto each other when dancing, and both sexes started a competition to see who could have the longest hair. All cut-off points are pretty arbitrary, but as a handy frame of reference, you could say that Sinatra's Rat Pack in Las Vegas in the early sixties represent the end of the hipster era as defined by this book. By 1968, four lovable moptops from Liverpool had decided that what rock 'n' roll really, really needed was a serious injection of brass band music and string quartets, and a hippie fan of theirs named Charles Manson out in California was turning on his Family to the White Album: "Are you hep to what the Beatles are saying? Helter Skelter is coming down. The Beatles are telling it like it is." Cab Calloway would have understood the use of the word "hep" in that last sentence, but he sure wouldn't have been likely to have gone up to any stray flower children on the street in Haight-Ashbury and asked them for the address of their tailor.

For the most part, though, it really doesn't matter very much whether you think *Ocean's Eleven* is the name of a football team, or that The Grifters were the vocal group who recorded "Save the Last Dance for Me." While it's probably true that the language used in films such as *High School Confidential* bears only a slight relation to the way that drug-crazed gang members actually spoke, it still has something of the authentic flavor of those times. Mostly though, it's just there to be enjoyed, and it's worth it just to imagine hordes of impressionable teenage filmgoers back in 1958 attempting to impress their dates with lines like "Give me an intro to this snake and I'll hitch up the reindeers for you."

Anyhow, I'd better hop in my kemp and take off for the casbah.

Plant ya now, dig ya later,

Max Décharné
Berlin, May 2000

Straight

from

the Fridge,

_____ Dad

A

A-1

The best, top of the heap
" 'That's my baby,' I said. 'We'll have our good times. Just you and me and thirty grand; maybe five or ten more if it's an A-1 job.' "
From the novel *Savage Night*,
Jim Thompson, 1953

A-Bomb juice

Moonshine liquor

A-OK

Fine, all in order, just right

A double this time, waiter. Your singles keep leaking.

The correct way to order drinks
From *Ocean's Eleven*, the novel of the film screenplay,
George Clayton Johnson and Jack Golden Russell, 1960

A shape in a drape

Someone who looks good in clothes, is sharply dressed

Abyssinia.

See you later. (I'll be seein' ya.)

Ace

1. Something superlative, the top
2. One dollar
3. A marijuana cigarette
4. A policeman
" 'Who's chasin' you, Frankie?'
'The aces. They're goin' to pin the sluggin' on me.' "
From the novel *The Man with the Golden Arm*,
Nelson Algren, 1949
5. "An outstanding, regular fellow."
From the booklet *The Jives of Doctor Hepcat*,
Lavada Durst, 1953

Ace in the hole

Something in reserve, an advantage; secret weapon, deriving from cardplayers having an ace up their sleeve
See the jazz recording "Ace in the Hole,"
The Black Diamond Seranaders, 1926.

Ace out	Cheat, defraud
Aces up	Something mighty fine, excellent
Action	What's happening, e.g., *"Where's the action, pops?"*
Adobe dollar	Mexican peso
Age of pain	Prohibition; the time of the 18th Amendment, which lasted from January 1920 until December 1933
Agitate the gravel	Leave, depart, vamoose
Ain't no sin to take off your skin, and dance around in your bones.	Enjoy yourself, get with it, relax.
Ain't nothin' you can tell me I don't already know.	I'm right, you're wrong, shut up.
Alabama lie detector	Police baton
All broke out with the blues	Depressed, low-down
All creeped up	Scared, apprehensive, frightened
All-electric	Far better looking than the average *"Ordinarily, too, I am not a guy who goes ga-ga on lamping a babe, even though, like this one, she makes it appear that other gals run on gas and she's an all-electric."* From the novel *Slab Happy*, Richard S. Prather, 1958
All gone	Drunk, intoxicated

All over them like a cheap suit	Sticking really close to someone, e.g., *"That guy at the dance was all over my sister like a cheap suit."*
All sharped up	Well dressed, suavely turned out
All shook up	Disturbed, hopped up, excited, real gone *"Cool down Eve, you look all shook up."* From the novel *Scandal High*, Herbert O. Pruett, 1960
All steamed up like a pants presser	Sexually excited
All wet	Disappointing, worthless
Alligator	1. *Down Beat's Yearbook of Swing, 1939*, lists this as "a swing fan who plays no instrument, or musician who frequents places where orchestras are playing." 2. Hipster term of address, often shortened to "gator." Similar in meaning to "cat" or "hepcat"
Already slated for crashville	Out of control, e.g., *"We could see that the car was already slated for crashville."*
Alreet	In order, fine, very good
Alroot	See "alreet."
Alvin	A rube, a sucker, an easy mark
Amscray	Run away, leave (pig latin for "scram")
Ankle	To walk
Ants in my pants	Sexually excited *"I'm gonna hug you baby good and tight, now love me baby like you done last night, cause I got ants*

in my pants,
baby for you . . ."
> From the blues recording "Ants in My Pants,"
> Bo Carter, 1931

Anywhere Possessing drugs,
e.g., *"Is you anywhere?" (Do you have any?)*
> From the autobiography *Really the Blues,*
> Mezz Mezzrow and Bernard Wolfe, 1946

Applesauce Flattery, insincere praise, a load of old flannel;
e.g., *"Don't hand me that applesauce, Pops."*

Ark "Dance hall, coliseum, any building for dances, meetings, etc."
> From the booklet *The Jives of Doctor Hepcat,*
> Lavada Durst, 1953

Artillery Guns

As bare as hell's backyard Completely empty

As busy as a one-legged tapdancer Extremely busy

As dead as five-cent beer Dead and buried

As drunk as two sailors Soused, plastered, three sheets to the wind

As full as a pair of goats Totally drunk
"Before long we were as full as a pair of goats."
> From the short story "The Golden Horseshoe,"
> Dashiell Hammett, 1920s

Ashes Having sex
e.g., *"Getting your ashes hauled."*
"She said I could haul her ashes
better than any other man,

she said I could sow my seed
anytime in her ash can."
> From "Ash Can Blues," Bob Clifford, c. 1930

"I worked all winter
and I worked all fall,
I've gotta wait until spring
to get my ashes hauled."
> From the blues recording "Tired As I Can Be,"
> Bessie Jackson (Lucille Bogan), 1934

> See also "Alleyman (Haul My Ashes)," Sadie Green,
> 1926 and "Looking for My Ash Hauler,"
> Washboard Sam, 1937.

Awash   Drunk

Axe   Musical instrument

B

B-girl   Bar girl, usually working in a clip joint, whose job
is to encourage the customers to buy more alcohol
"Settling down in Baltimore, she found lucrative
and undemanding work as a B-Girl. Or, more
accurately, it was undemanding as far as she was
concerned. Lilly Dillon wasn't putting out for
anyone; not, at least, for a few bucks or drinks."
> From the novel *The Grifters,* Jim Thompson, 1963

Baby blues   Eyes

Back door man   Lover; someone who sneaks in through the back
door when the husband is away
> See "I'm a Front Door Woman with a Back Door
> Man," a blues recording by Lillian Glinn, 1929.

Bad   1. Good
2. Evil

Bag	Your interests, your preferences or habitual doings
Bag man	Go-between, drug dealer, person to whom protection money is paid
Ball the jack	1. To move fast

Ball the jack

1. To move fast
"Suppose you were riding that manifest out of Denton, the fast meat train that balls the jack all the way into El Reno."
>From the novel *Savage Night*, Jim Thompson, 1953

2. Having sex
" 'I was pretty obnoxious myself,' Deedee giggled. 'I mean, I don't really think you and Moms were balling the jack together. You know that, Brad.' "
>From the novel *Run Tough, Run Hard*,
>Carson Bingham, 1961

3. Have a wild time, get real gone
>See "Ballin' the Jack," a recording by The Victor Military Band, 1914. (The following year they recorded a title called "Blame It on the Blues.") See also "Ballin' the Jack," recorded by The Louisiana Rhythm Kings, 1929.

Bam   Girlfriend, steady date, parking pet

Band rats   Groupies

Bar-polisher   Habitual drinker, frequenter of gin-joints

Barbecue   Girlfriend, good-looking woman
"She faced him now, her eyes blazing, her face flushed. 'I don't think I particularly enjoyed your role the night of the party, either, if you want the honest truth about it, Brad Dixon! Strutting off with that blond barbecue the minute you set foot in the house!' "
>From the novel *Run Tough, Run Hard*,
>Carson Bingham, 1961

Louis Armstrong's Hot Five released a jazz record called "Struttin' with Some Barbecue" in 1927; i.e., dancing with a pretty girl.

Barbecue stool   The electric chair

Barfly — Regular drinker, gin mill cowboy, serious lush-head

> See "Bill the Bar Fly," a country record by
> Tex Ritter, 1935.

Barrel fever — Drunkenness, a raging thirst

Barrelhouse —
1. Gin-joint, taproom, speakeasy, brothel
> See jazz recordings "Barrel House Man,"
> Elzadie Robinson, 1926 and "Barrel House Man,"
> Will Ezell, 1927.
2. Style of boogie piano playing
> *Down Beat's Yearbook of Swing, 1939*, calls it
> "Swing music played in a 'dirty and lowdown'
> style."

Batter the drag — Beg on the street

Battle axe — Musician's slang for a trumpet

Beanery — No-nonsense food joint

Beastly — Very good

Beat —
1. Exhausted, worn out
> *"Art sounded more than tired, he sounded beat."*
> > From the novel *The Golden Key*,
> > William O'Farrell, 1962
2. Broke, out of cash, tapsville
3. Hipster of the late 1940s and 1950s defined by the literary group around Kerouac, Ginsberg, Corso, etc.
> *"The night was getting more and more frantic. I wished Dean and Carlo were there—then realized they'd be out of place and unhappy.*
>
> *They were like the man with the dungeon stone and the gloom, rising from the underground, the sordid hipsters of America, a new beat generation that I was slowly joining."*
> > From the novel *On the Road*,
> > Jack Kerouac, 1957
4. To steal

Beat it out. Play it hot; emphasize the rhythm.

Beat me Daddy, eight-to-the-bar. Play some boogie-woogie for me.
The left-hand bass lines in typical boogie-woogie piano feature a driving, eight-to-the-bar rhythm.
"In a little honky-tonky village in Texas
There's a guy who plays the best piano by far,
He can play piano any way you like it,
But the kind he likes the best is eight-to-the-bar."
> From the boogie-woogie recording
> "Beat Me Daddy, Eight to the Bar,"
> The Will Bradley Trio, 1942

Beat someone for their bread Swindle or rob someone
"I knew the cab driver had beat me for my bread, but there was no use crying, it was gone."
> From the autobiography *I, Paid My Dues, Good Times . . . No Bread, A Story of Jazz,*
> Babs Gonzales, 1967

Beat the boards Tap-dance

Beat the gong Smoke opium

Beat the rap Escape criminal charges, be found not-guilty
> Frederick L. Nebel wrote a story called "Beat the Rap" for the May 1931 issue of *Black Mask* magazine.

Beat the tubs Play the drums
"It's all in the wrist n' I got the touch—dice, stud or with a cue. I even beat the tubs a little 'cause that's in the wrist too. Here—pick a card."
> Frankie Machine lists his accomplishments.
> From the novel *The Man with the Golden Arm,*
> Nelson Algren, 1949

Beat your chops Talk
"Say, is it a solid fact that you guys can beat your chops, lace the boots, and knock the licks out groovy as a movie whilst jiving in a comin'-on fashion?"
> Bing Crosby to Nat Cole, U.S. radio, 1945

Beat your gums   Talk
"You know, medicine's found ways to prolong some old squares' lives. You know how they spend it? Beating their gums . . ."
    From the film *Shake, Rattle and Rock,* 1957

Beatnik   A word coined by Herb Caen of the *San Fransisco Chronicle* in 1958, for an article about the Beats. Sputnik, the Russian satellite, was much in the news at the time. Picked up by the media it came to symbolize to the public the jazz-loving, Kerouac-reading, nonconformists of the 1950s, but was a term hated by many of the Beats themselves.
"She had her old beatnik costume on—the tight black pants, the bulky black sweater—and her hair was brushed and her lipstick was bright and straight."
    From the novel *The Wrecking Crew,*
    Donald Hamilton, 1960

    See the vocal group recording "Beatnik Girl,"
    The Bi-Tones, 1960.

Bebop   Modern jazz style developed by Charlie Parker, Dizzy Gillespie, and others in the early 1940s
Dizzy put out a single called "Bebop" in 1945.
    See also "He Beeped When He Shoulda Bopped,"
    Dizzy Gillespie and his Orchestra, 1946; "Poppa
    Stoppa's (Bebop Blues)," Mr. Google Eyes and his
    Four Bars, 1949; "BeBop Wino," a vocal group
    recording by The Lamplighters, 1953.

Bedroom furniture   Dame, doll, gasser;
e.g., *"She's a swell piece of bedroom furniture."*

Beef   1. Complaint, grievance
"I'm not beefing about the Saratoga let-down. The guys we were fishing for just didn't bite."
    From the novel *Killers Don't Care,*
    Rod Callahan, 1950
2. To talk
3. A criminal charge or a crime

Behind	Under the influence of something
Behind the cork	Drunk, intoxicated
Behind the eight-ball	In trouble, in a difficult spot " 'I thought Augie was a particular friend of yours.' 'I thought so, too. And here he puts me behind the eight-ball with you . . .' " From the novel *Little Men, Big World*, W. R. Burnett, 1951
Behind the parade	Old hat, outdated, passé
Behind the stick	Working behind a bar—the stick being the wooden bar-top itself
Belly fiddle	Guitar
Belly gun	Weapon with a short barrel, usually a 32.20, used for shooting someone at very close range
Bellyache	Complain, e.g., *"What are you bellyaching about?"*
Belt of booze	A drink
Belting the grape	Drinking wine
Bend someone's ear	Talk, chatter *"Anyway, thanks for the cheer, I hope you didn't mind my bending your ear."* From the ballad "One for My Baby (and One More for the Road)," Frank Sinatra, live at The Sands, Las Vegas, 1966
Bent out of shape	1. Upset, disturbed 2. High on drugs or drink
Berries	Something mighty fine *"She had black hair an' black eyes an' a figure that looked like a serpent with nerve troubles. Except for the fact that she hadn't had her face lifted she*

mighta been your favourite film star.
That baby was the berries."
> From the novel *Your Deal, My Lovely,*
> Peter Cheyney, 1941

Better tune me in and get my signal right Understand what I'm telling you
"Better tune me in and get my signal right
Or there'll be no rockin' tomorrow night."
> From the rockabilly recording
> "I Got a Rocket in My Pocket," Jimmy Logsdon
> (a.k.a. Jimmy Lloyd), 1958

Bible-puncher Clergyman

Big barracuda An important guy
" 'Got his name?'
'Morrison—big barracuda.'
'He was D.O.A. Knife cut his heart in half.'
'Nobody did it, nobody saw it.' "
> From the film *Where the Sidewalk Ends,* 1950

Big chill Death

Big house Prison
> In nineteenth-century England, it was a slang
> name for the workhouse.

Big house up the river Sing Sing prison

Big sleep Death
> Used by Raymond Chandler as the title of one
> of his most famous books, published in 1939,
> and filmed in 1946 with Humphrey Bogart as
> Philip Marlowe.

Biscuit snatchers Fingers, hands

Biters Teeth

Blab Talk, give the game away

Blab sheet Newspaper

Black	Nighttime
	"Say, you look ready as Mister Freddy this black."
	Freddy Slack talks hep to Ella Mae Morse
	during the intro to their 1946 boogie recording
	"House of Blue Lights."
Black and white	Police car
Blackstick	Clarinet
Blast	Telephone call
	"If you ever come to Riverport, how about giving me a blast on the phone?"
	From the film *Jailhouse Rock,* 1957
Blast the joint	Smoke dope
Blast yourself wacky	Go mad
Blasted	Drunk, intoxicated
Blasting party	Dope party
Bleating your trap	Complaining
Blind staggers	Drunkenness
Blocked	Drunk or high on drugs
Blonde	*"It was a blonde. A blonde to make a bishop kick a hole in a stained glass window."*
	From the novel *Farewell, My Lovely,* Raymond Chandler, 1940
Blot out	Kill, assassinate
Blow	General term for playing a musical instrument, regardless of type
Blow a fuse	Go crazy, go wild
Blow in on the scene	Arrive, make an entrance

Blow the box   Play the piano

Blow the joint   Leave the building
"Let's blow this joint, the music's dead . . ."
From the rockabilly recording "Cast Iron Arm,"
Johnny Peanuts Wilson, 1956

Blow the scene   Leave, disappear
"Look, baby, just don't you blow the scene on me!
Stick in town or I'll chase you down to hell itself!"
From the novel *Two Timing Tart,*
John Davidson, 1961

Blow the works   Spill the beans, tell all

Blow up a storm   Cut loose during a musical number, get hot, play
at your best
"Say Fats, a bunch of the kids would like to listen
to you blowin' up a storm. Would you let them
listen in?"
From the film *Shake, Rattle and Rock,* 1957

See also the jazz novel *Blow Up a Storm,*
Garson Kanin, 1959.

Blow your jets   Get annoyed, lose your cool

Blowtop   1. A crazy or violent person, someone with a short
temper
2. "Fellows who are excellent in their fields
especially music and dancing."
From the booklet *The Jives of Doctor Hepcat,*
Lavada Durst, 1953.

"Ain't that going to be kicks . . . listen will you to this
old tenorman blow his top."
From the novel *On the Road,* Jack Kerouac, 1957

Boat   Automobile
"Capone motioned at a glossy black convertible job
parked curbside. 'That your boat?'"
From the novel *Al Capone,* John Roeburt, 1959

13

Bobby-soxer   Teenage girl, much given to screaming at
Frank Sinatra
> The name derives from the fashion for wearing
> short white socks.

Body scissors   Having sex
> *"I knew by now that she was the kind of dame you
> couldn't turn your back on for five minutes without
> her having a body scissors on somebody."*
> From the novel *Kiss Tomorrow Goodbye*,
> Horace McCoy, 1949

Boil my cabbage   Blues slang for sex, much used by the female blues
singers of the 1920s
> *"He boiled my first cabbage
> and he made it awful hot,
> he boiled my first cabbage
> and he made it awful hot,
> when he put in the bacon
> it overflowed the pot."*
> From "Empty Bed Blues Part 2,"
> Bessie Smith, 1928

> See also the blues recordings "Anybody Here Want
> to Try My Cabbage?", Maggie Jones, 1924; "Good
> Cabbage," Victoria Spivey, 1937.

Boiler   Automobile
> *"We're still talking when this boiler screeches up
> and stops on a dime. Out pops Cooch and walks
> towards us."*
> From the short story "The Rites of Death,"
> Hal Ellson, 1956

**Boloney
or Baloney**   Lies
> *"A bundle of first-class boloney straight off the ice."*
> From the novel *Can Ladies Kill?*,
> Peter Cheyney, 1938

Bomb   1. Automobile
> *"Give a listen. Power man! What a bomb!"*
> From the novel *Go, Man. Go!*,
> Edward De Roo, 1959

*"That red Thunderbird
is the craziest bomb in town ..."*
> From "Red Thunderbird," a rock 'n' roll recording
> by Lynn Howard and The Accents, 1958

2. A failure, such as a musical or
theatrical performance

Bone orchard   Cemetery
> See "Bone Orchard Blues," a blues recording by
> Ida Cox, 1928.

Boneyard   1. Cemetery
> See "Boneyard Shuffle," a country recording by The
> Arkansas Travellers, 1927.

2. Auto repair shop, garage
*"It's in the boneyard, Molly ... you know, the
boneyard where the elephants go when they're tired
of living." (I've smashed up the car.)*
> From the novel *Run Tough, Run Hard,*
> Carson Bingham, 1961.

Booster   Shoplifter

**Boots laced
up tight**   Hep, righteous, in the know, a suave customer

Booze fight   A drinking spree
> There was a biker gang called the Booze Fighters in
> Los Angeles just after World War II.

Bop   1. To fight
> The gang fights in the 1960 film *The Young Savages*
> are called "bops" rather than "rumbles."

2. To dance
*"When I die don't bury me at all,
Just nail my bones up on the wall,
Beneath these bones let these words be seen:
'The running gears of a boppin' machine.'"*
> From "Rockin' Bones," a rockabilly recording by
> Ronnie Dawson, 1958

3. Jazz movement originating in the 1940s
> The word "bebop" was shortened to "bop" with
> Charlie Parker's 1947 recording "Bongo Bop."

"At this time, 1947, bop was going like mad all over America. The fellows at the Loop blew, but with a tired air, because bop was somewhere between its Charlie Parker Ornithology period and another period that began with Miles Davis."
From *On the Road,* Jack Kerouac, 1957.

See "Coppin' the Bop," Jay Jay Johnson's BeBoppers, 1946 and "Bop's Your Uncle," George Shearing, 1947.

Jazzman Babs Gonzales had a band in 1946 called Babs' Three Bips and a Bop. Artie Shaw opened a club in New York in 1949 called Bop City.

"See you tomorrow, cats. Same time, same channel, same bop beat . . ."
From the film *Shake, Rattle and Rock,* 1957.

Bop kick   "To play the new sound in music, the latest dance step."
From the booklet *The Jives of Doctor Hepcat,* Lavada Durst, 1953

Born tired   Lazy

Born under a bad sign   Fated, unlucky

Boss   Something really good, the best

Bottle babies   Drunks
From the autobiography *Really the Blues,* Mezz Mezzrow and Bernard Wolfe, 1946

In the short story collection The Neon Wilderness (1947) Nelson Algren has the variant "bottle boy": "And the simple everyday bottle boy, who fights when he drinks, and he drinks all the time."

Bottle heister   A drunkard

Bottle tipper   Heavy drinker
>>> See "The Fiddlin' Bootleggers," a country recording by The Monroe County Bottle Tippers, 1928.

Bottle up and go   Hit the trail, cut out, vamoose, take a powder
>>> See "Bottle Up and Go," a vocal group recording by The Enchanters, 1957.

Bottom dealer   Swindler, someone who deals cards from the bottom of the deck

Bought and sold and done for   Broke, down on your luck

Box   1. Vagina
>>> See the shy, romantic 1950s vocal group performance "Baby Let Me Bang Your Box" by The Bangers, or "Hot Box Is on My Mind," a piano blues by Kingfish Bill Tomlin, 1929.

2. A safe
"Can you bust a box if you have to?" i.e., *Can you crack a safe?*
>>> From the novel *Carny Kill*, Robert Edmond Alter, 1966

3. Record player or phonograph

Bozo   1. Idiot, square
>>> Originating from Bozo the Clown, a type of circus performer whose main distinguishing characteristic is stupidity.

2. Ordinary guy, all purpose term of address, e.g., *"She is wearin' a lime-green frock that was cut by a bozo that could wield a mean pair of shears."*

Bracelets   Handcuffs
"One of the uniformed cops frisks me and snaps a pair of bracelets on my wrists."
>>> From the novel *Killers Don't Care*, Rod Callahan, 1950

Brain it around   Think it over

Brass rail   Bar or saloon

Brawl	Wild party
Bread	1. Money *"In the bread department I am nowhere . . ."* 　　From the film *High School Confidential,* 1958 2. Penis 　　See "She's Your Cook, But She Burns My Bread 　　Sometimes," a blues recording by Bo Carter, 1930.
Bread pan	Vagina *"She makes my bread rise late hours in the night, I put my bread right in her pan and I shoves it clean out of sight."* 　　From "Bread Pan (Just My Size)," a piano blues by 　　Roosevelt Sykes, 1937
Bread stasher	Working stiff, wage slave, someone who saves for a rainy day
Breadsville	A bank
Break it down	1. Musical term, defined by *Down Beat's Yearbook of Swing,* 1939, as "To get hot, swing it, go to town." 2. Spill the beans, speak your piece " *'I'm listening,' he said. 'Break it down.'* " 　　From the novel *Death Is Confidential,* 　　Lawrence Lariar, 1959
Break it off	Stop talking
Break out like the measles	Go wild, play hot music, swing it
Breakfast uptown	A night in jail
Breathing natural gas	Hep, alert, knowing the score
Breeze	Leave, possibly in a hurry; e.g., *"Think I'd better breeze . . ."*
Brew	An alcoholic drink

Bright	Daytime
Bright disease	To know too much
Bringdown	Something or someone depressing
Broadway battleship	New York streetcar
Brush	To ignore someone
Bucket	Prison *"I'll stay under cover. He's too stir-wise for me. I smell of the bucket."* i.e., *(He is sure to be able to tell that I've just come out of prison.)* From the short story "Goldfish," Raymond Chandler, 1936
Bucket of blood	Cheap bar, spit and sawdust joint See "Bucket of Blood," a piano blues by Will Ezell, 1929.
Bucket of suds	Take-away beer, carried home in a bucket
Bug	To annoy or irritate *"I'm sorry, baby, but don't bug me."* From the film *The Killers*, 1956 "See Like, You Bug Me," a vocal group recording by The Quarter Notes, 1958.
Bug juice	Moonshine liquor
Buggy	1. Automobile 2. Crazy, short for bughouse (See next entry.) *"Take your buggy boy friend and clear out of here before I forget I'm a lady."* From the novel *Pop 1280*, Jim Thompson, 1964
Bughouse	Crazy, insane, lost it completely *The mob nickname Bugsy derives from this—a crazy guy, a stone killer.*

Washington Square in Chicago has long been known as Bughouse Square, as has Union Square in New York.

Build me a drink	Mix me a cocktail.
Built	Someone with a good figure " 'You've got six weeks to make her a star.' 'Easy, Fats, it takes time. Rome wasn't built in a day.' 'She ain't Rome . . .' " i.e., *She's built already.* From the film *The Girl Can't Help It*, 1956
Bull	Cop, policeman
Bull fiddle	Double bass
Bulletproof	Completely drunk
Bulling	Something good, mighty fine
Bum steer	A bad deal, something wrong, an unlucky break
Bump	To kill
Bump your gums	Talk a lot
Bunco artist	Con man, swindler
Bundle	Bankroll, a quantity of money

Bunk habit	*"The practice of lounging around while others smoke opium, and inhaling the fumes."*
	    From the autobiography *Really the Blues*,
	    Mezz Mezzrow and Bernard Wolfe, 1946

Burg	Town, city
Buried	1. As drunk as a skunk, plastered 2. A life sentence in jail
Burn	1. Die in the electric chair

2. Kill someone
*"Max grinned genially. From his jacket
pocket he produced a small-calibre pistol,
then dropped it back again. 'We want you
to burn him, Rick.'
Rick stared at him with slowly growing
comprehension. 'You mean kill him?'
he finally asked in a husky voice.
'You got the scoop,' Max said."*
> From the short story "A Hood Is Born,"
> Richard Deming, 1959

Burn leather
1. Dance
> See "The Joint Is Jumping," a jazz recording by
> Fats Waller, 1937.
2. Walk fast or run

Burn me up
Go on, give it all you've got
*"Burn me up this time, let's see if we can get a little
fire into it."*
> Elvis to his musicians. From the film
> *Jailhouse Rock,* 1957

Burn my clothes
An expression of surprise
*"Burn my clothes if it isn't Romeo, our financial
backer."*
> From the film *Dames,* 1934

Burn rubber
1. Drive fast, make a quick getaway
2. Have sex

Burned
1. Annoyed
2. Robbed
3. Killed

Burning with a low blue flame
Drunk, swimming, sluiced to the gills

Bus
Car

Busier than a hustler with two bunks
Extremely busy

Bust your conk	Work hard, be thorough
Bust your vest	Be big, magnanimous

Busted	1. Arrested
	2. Broke, poverty-stricken
	"I'm busted, flat."
	    From the novel *Red Harvest*,
	    Dashiell Hammett, 1929

Busted flush	Bankrupt
Busting into a can	Cracking a safe
Butcher shop	Hospital
Butt me	Give me a cigarette

Butter-and-egg man	Out-of-town big spender, the backer of a theater show, free with his money and often a sucker
	    See "Big Butter and Egg Man from the West," a
	    jazz recording by Louis Armstrong's Hot Five,
	    1927.

Button	The lookout in a criminal operation
Button-buster	A braggart or loudmouth
Button your gabber.	Shut up.
Button your lip.	Keep quiet.
Buy the farm	To die, peg out, cash in your chips
Buzz	To rob, to pick someone's pocket *"Tell you what I'll do, Tiger. I'll give you the names* *of eight cannons that fit the job and I'll bet you* *thirty-eight dollars and fifty cents that one of them* *buzzed this moll's wallet."* From the film *Pickup on South Street*, 1953

Buzz me.   Give me a call on the telephone.
"Buzz me, buzz me, buzz me baby,
I'm waitin' for your call . . ."
From "Buzz Me," an R&B jump-jive recording by
Louis Jordan and The Tympany Five, 1946

See also "Buzz Me Babe," a blues recording by Slim
Harpo, 1960.

Buzzer   Badge or ID, usually that of the police

C

C-jag   Cocaine binge
Cornell Woolrich wrote a story called "C-Jag" for
the October 1940 issue of *Black Mask* magazine, in
which the murderer can't remember what he's
done with the body due to an over-indulgence of
snow.

C note   One hundred dollars
"In a moment, Colosimo returned. He thrust money
at Capone with a flourish. 'Five Cs, for a stake.' "
From the novel *Al Capone*, John Roeburt, 1959

Cabbage   1. Money
"I'm looking for some guys with lots of cabbage and
a certain amount of respectability . . . worth shaking
down."
From the novel *Murder on Monday*, Robert Patrick
Wilmot, 1952
2. 1920s blues slang for genitals

Cackle factory   Lunatic asylum
" 'He'd be just the man who might try to con
Torelli.'
'Con Torelli! You must have been sprung
from the cackle factory. Not even Gunner
would try that.' "
From the novel *Darling, It's Death*,
Richard S. Prather, 1953

23

Café sunburn Pallor
From the autobiography *Really the Blues*,
Mezz Mezzrow and Bernard Wolfe, 1946

Cake cutter Short-change artist, swindler

Calaboose Prison
"The judge he pondered,
Then turned me loose, sayin'
'Too many winos in my calaboose.' "
From the hillbilly boogie recording "The Wino
Boogie," Bill Nettles, 1954

Call some hogs Snore

Camisole Prison slang for a straitjacket

Can 1. Prison
"I'm fresh out of prison
Six years in the can . . ."
From the country recording "Drink Up and Go
Home," Carl Perkins, 1955
2. Automobile
" 'Tony,' said Rico, 'ditch that can and come back for
your split.' " i.e., (Dispose of the getaway car and
then we'll divide up the money.)
From the novel *Little Caesar*, W. R. Burnett, 1929
3. Backside, rear end
"Ira Borch—the grinning stranger, a slimy
sonofabitch who'd been on my can for six months."
From the novel *Always Leave 'Em Dying*,
Richard S. Prather, 1961

Can it. Shut up.
" 'Mike, you surprise me. I thought you
were keen on equal rights and all that jazz.'
'Can it,' he growled. 'You know where I
stand at this late date.' "
From the novel *The Bedroom Bolero*,
Michael Avallone, 1963

Canary　1. Female singer
*"You once had a great nose for finding new talent.
Dug up some big canaries, but the booze got
in your way."*
　　　From the film *The Girl Can't Help It*, 1956

*There were also many recordings of real canaries in
the 1930s, often trained to whistle popular tunes of
the day. "There must be a steady sale for 'actual
canary bird recordings' somewhere, for there is
seldom a month without at least one release by
feathered warblers . . ."*
　　　From the magazine *Phonograph Monthly Review*,
　　　New York, November 1930
2. Police informer

**Cancel
someone's
Christmas**　Kill them

Canned heat　Cheap hooch made from a mixture of alcohol and
methylated spirits, much favored by hoboes and
winos
　　　See the blues recording "Canned Heat Blues,"
　　　Sloppy Henry, 1928.

Cannon　1. Gun, firearm
2. Gunman
*". . . . Dave Moroni, Moron for short, who had been
a minor cog in Murder, Inc. when Bugsy Siegel had
been one of their top torpedoes. The other guy was a
top-notch cannon who could kiss the dog and lift
your wrist watch between ticks."*
　　　From the novel *Darling, It's Death*,
　　　Richard S. Prather, 1953

In the film Pickup on South Street *(1953), the
word is frequently used to describe a pickpocket or
petty criminal.*

**Can't see a hole
in a ladder**　Completely drunk

Cap　To shoot someone

| Caper | Robbery, criminal enterprise |

| Capper | A shill, one who assists a cardsharp in swindling the suckers |

| Carve your knob | "To make you know, understand."
From the booklet *The Jives of Doctor Hepcat*, Lavada Durst, 1953 |

| Cash in your checks | Die
"For the files, Blackie Gitz is just a mobster who cashed in his checks, via three slugs in his back, said slugs being non-self-inflicted."
From the novel *The Corrupt Ones*, J. C. Barton, c. 1950 |

| Cat | Dude, hipster, a righteous groover
In 1953, Doctor Hepcat defined a cat as "a young man who is part of the modern social whirl, dresses in latest smart styles, understands all types of music, dances, and is accepted." |

*"There's a cat in town that you might know,
he goes by the name of Domino.
A long key chain and a diamond ring,
a blue sports car, he's a crazy king."*
From the rockabilly recording, "Domino," Roy Orbison, 1956

See the jazz recording "That Cat Is High," Tommy Powell and his Hi-De-Ho Boys, 1936

See also the R&B jump-jive recording "At the Swing Cats Ball," Louis Jordan and The Tympany Five, 1939.

Not surprisingly, Down Beat's Yearbook of Swing, 1939, *defines Cats as "musicians in a swing orchestra, or people who like swing music."*
See also the jazz recording "Stop the War (The Cats Are Killin' Themselves)," Wingy Manone and his Orchestra, 1941.

Cat clothes	Hipster threads—serious clothing, not for the squares
	See the rockabilly recording "Put Your Cat Clothes On," Carl Perkins, 1956.
Cathouse	Brothel
Cat's pajamas	The best, top of the heap
Catch a handful of boxcars	Hop a freight train and leave town
Catting around	Playing the field, philandering
Caught in a snowstorm	Addicted to cocaine
Century	One hundred dollars
Chalk-eater	A gambler who always backs the favorite in a horse race
Charging a bank	Robbing a bank
	"Kid, we got us a little bank in Cedars just itchin' to be charged. It's all cased properly."
	From the film *They Live by Night*, 1948
Chassis	Body, limbs, etc.
Chat 'n' chew	Restaurant, hash house
Cheaters	Eyeglasses, spectacles
Check the beat	Listen to the music
Check the character	Look at that person over there
	From the film *High School Confidential*, 1958
Chew the scenery	Overact, make a big deal of something
Chicago lightning	Gunfire
Chicago overcoat	Coffin

Chicago piano   Machine gun

Chick   Girl, dame
"Dean had arrived the night before, the first time in New York, with his beautiful little sharp chick Marylou."
> From the novel *On the Road*, Jack Kerouac, 1957

*"Let me tell you bout my real gone chick,
She's got a different style . . ."*
> From the rockabilly recording "Tongue-Tied Jill,"
> Charlie Feathers, 1956

> See the vocal group recording "That Chick's Too Young to Fry," The Deep River Boys, 1945. (Also covered by The Prisonaires, from the Tennessee State Penitentiary, some of whom had wound up behind bars for exactly the reasons spelled out in the song.)

Chicken dinner   Pretty young girl
> From the autobiography *Really the Blues*,
> Mezz Mezzrow and Bernard Wolfe, 1946

Chicken ranch   Brothel

Chicken run   Russian-roulette style race with cars

Chill   1. Kill, assassinate
2. Stop that, wait a minute

Chill your chat.   Stop talking.

Chime   The time of day, the hour

Chippy   1. Part-time prostitute
"My God! What did I ever think of to put in with a chippy like you?"
> From the novel *The High Window*,
> Raymond Chandler, 1943

> See the jazz recording "Chasin' Chippies," Cootie Williams and his Rug Cutters, 1938.
2. Occasional user of drugs

Chirp	Female vocalist
Chiseler	Swindler, cheat
Chiv	Knife
Choke dog	Rough moonshine liquor
Chop-beatin' session	Discussion

Chop suey	1. A messy death
	"Some of the nicest people you ever took a gander at suddenly go daffy and make chop suey out of their best friends, with a meat axe."
	  From the film *Sleep, My Love*
	2. Having sex
	  See the blues recording "Who'll Chop Your Suey When I'm Gone?," Willie Jackson, 1926.

Chopper	Machine gun, or machine-gunner
Choppers	Teeth
Chops	Any part of the body a musician uses to play his instrument
Chow	Food
Chuck	Food
Chuck horrors	Extreme reaction to food brought on by drug withdrawal
Chump change	Small change, a moderate amount of money, low wages
Cinder dicks	Railroad police
Clam up	Keep quiet, fall silent
Clam yourself.	Be quiet; shut up.

Clams	Dollars
	"Nothin' a million clams won't cure." Danny Ocean gets optimistic, from *Ocean's Eleven,* the novelization of the film screenplay, George Clayton Johnson and Jack Golden Russell, 1960
Claret	Blood
Claws	Fingers
Claws sharp	"The act of being well informed on all subjects." From the booklet *The Jives of Doctor Hepcat,* Lavada Durst, 1953
Clean	1. Unarmed 2. Not carrying any stolen goods
Cliff-dweller	Resident of a high-rise apartment block
Climb the six-foot ladder	To die, be buried
Clip	1. Kill someone 2. Punch someone *"A guy in the bar come at me with a bottle.* *I clipped him good, and he busted his head on the* *bar railing."* From the novel *Odds Against Tomorrow,* William P. McGivern, 1957 3. Cheat someone
Clip joint	Club, bar, or other business which routinely swindles its customers
Clipster	Confidence man
Clout	1. Influence, authority 2. To steal
Clouting heaps	Stealing cars
Clown	Idiot, square, a waste of space
Clued-in	Aware, knowledgeable, on top of the situation

Clutch buster	Hot-rodder
Clyde	A square, a hick, a goon from Straightsville
Coal bin	Blues slang for a vagina

"*I'll take your order*
and fill your bin,
so get it cleaned out
and I'll put it right in,
'cause I'm just a coal man
sellin' the hottest stuff in town."
> From the blues recording "The Hottest Stuff in
> Town," Bob Howe and Frankie Griggs, 1935

Cockroach joint	Cheap restaurant
Coffee grinder	Classic striptease act
Coffin nails	Cigarettes

"*Get outta here with your coffin nails*
Can't you see you're on the wrong trail,
Go 'way, boy, don't wanna see one lit
Or I'll go into a nicotine fit."
> From the country recording "Nicotine Fit,"
> Mississippi Slim, 1954

Coffin varnish	Rough liquor
Cold meat cart	Hearse
Cold meat party	A funeral

> From the novel *Halo in Blood*,
> Howard Browne, 1946

Cold storage	Prison
Collar	1. To arrest someone 2. To acquire something
Comb your knowledge box	Comb your hair

Combed	Searched, frisked
	"If a prowl went past, the coppers would
	comb them sure."
	    From the novel *Little Men, Big World*,
	    W. R. Burnett, 1951

Come apart like a two-bit suitcase	Lose it, fall to pieces, dissolve into tears
Come clean	Tell all, speak up, confess *Jazz pioneer Buddy Bolden regularly played a venue* *in New Orleans around the year 1900 called Come* *Clean Hall. "You'd better talk George, come clean.* *Either you talk, or we'll get it out of the girl."* From the film *The Killing*, 1956
Come to life	Get real, face the truth
Comin' on	Hep, in control, confident; like a performer coming onstage and making an entrance
Coney Island whitefish	Used condom floating in the sea
Continental	A damn, a curse e.g., *"I don't give a continental . . ."*
Cooch dancing	Hootchie-cooching, burlesque dancing, stripping
Cook	To do something well
Cookie cutter	Policeman's badge

Cool	1. In the know, A-OK, hep
	2. Unworried, calm, relaxed
	    See the jazz recording "How You Gonna Keep
	    Kool?," The Georgia Melodians, 1924.
	
	That same year in the Presidential elections, Calvin
	Coolidge used the slogan "Keep Cool with Coolidge."
	    See also the jazz recordings "Look Hot, Keep Cool,"
	    The Harmonians; 1933; and "Keep Cool, Fool,"
	    Les Brown and His Orchestra, 1941.

Cool, calm, and a solid wig	Someone suave, a hepcat, a groover
Cool cat	A dude, a hipster, a real gone daddy

"*Ubangi stomp with a rock 'n' roll,
beats anything that you ever been told.
Ubangi stomp, Ubangi style,
when it hits it drives a cool cat wild . . .*"
> From the rockabilly recording "Ubangi Stomp,"
> Warren Smith, 1956

Cool it. Calm down, don't worry, don't make a fuss.

"*They're ready to fight, but Elmo cuts in, 'Cool it, you studs,' he tells them. 'I said cool it!' *"
> From the short story "The Rites of Death,"
> Hal Ellson, 1956

See also the rock 'n' roll song "Cool It, Baby" by Eddie Fontaine, as featured in the 1956 film *The Girl Can't Help It*, which contains the immortal lines:

"*I love your eyes, I love your lips,
They taste even better than potato chips.*"

Cooler Prison cell, solitary confinement

Cop To obtain

Cop a drear Die, expire, cash in your chips

Cop a nod Go to sleep

Cop a plea Plea bargain in order to get a lower sentence
> See the jazz recording "Coppin' a Plea,"
> Gene Krupa and His Orchestra, 1941.

Cop a slave Get a job

Cop a sneak Surreptitious look

Cop a squat Sit down

Cop an attitude	Behave in a negative or aggressive fashion
Cop and blow.	Easy come, easy go. You win some, you lose some. *"He reconciled himself to the name of the game. Cop and blow."* From the autobiography *I, Paid My Dues*, Babs Gonzales, 1967
Copasetic	Good, in order, everything alright, sometimes spelled "copacetic" *"The highest compliment in the hep world, anything you can do you are a master of it."* From the booklet *The Jives of Doctor Hepcat*, Lavada Durst, 1953
Corn squeezings	Moonshine liquor *"Mighty, mighty pleasin' Pappy's corn squeezings, mmm . . . white lightnin'."* From the rockabilly song "White Lightning," George Jones, 1959
Cornball style	Square, boring, clichéd
Corn-fed	From the country, coarse, unsophisticated
Cosmic goo	Metaphysics *"Don't worry me with all that cosmic goo, I've got practical problems."* From the novel *Blow Up a Storm*, Garson Kanin, 1959
County hotel	Local jail
Crack some suds	Drink beer
Crack the books	Read
Crack wise	Joke, talk back, be sarcastic
Crack your jaw	Talk
Crap out	Be unlucky, fail

Crapshoot	A risky business, chancy undertaking
Crash-out	Prison break *Sometimes spoken as "crush out." (To "crush," in nineteenth-century English slang, meant to run away.)*
Crashing the ether	Broadcasting on the radio
Crazy	Good, superlative, wild, the best *"Ooh man, dig those crazy lips Ooh man, boy she really flips, Ooh man, dig that crazy chick."*

> From the R&B jump-jive recording "Dig That Crazy Chick," Sam Butera and The Witnesses, 1958

> See also the rock 'n' roll recording "Crazy, Man, Crazy," Bill Haley and The Comets, 1954.

Richard S. Prather, author of numerous crime novels in the 1950s featuring private eye Shell Scott, once wrote a book called Dig That Crazy Grave. *During the course of his million-selling career he also treated the public to* The Scrambled Yeggs, Have Gat Will Travel, *and* The Wailing Frail.

Crease	1. To shoot *"Someone decided to crease Travis. He was shot last night."*

> From the novel *You Can Always Duck,* Peter Cheyney, 1943

2. To hit or to stun

Creep-joint	Brothel where the customers are likely to have their pockets picked
Crib	1. Home, apartment, residence 2. A safe
Croak	Die
Croak sheet	Life insurance policy

Croaker	1. Doctor " 'Is Burns bad?' 'Yeah, but the croaker says he'll survive.' " From the novel *The Fast Buck*, James Hadley Chase, 1952 2. Murderer, i.e., one who croaks someone
Crocked	Drunk
Croonette	Female singer
Cross-eyed	Drunk
Crowd-pleaser	Police gun
Cruiser	Automobile
Cruising for a bruising	Looking for trouble *"Cruising—looking for my gal* *I'm cruising—goin' don't know where* *I'm cruising—looking for my gal* *I'm cruising for a bruising that man with* *her is gonna get . . ."* From the rock 'n' roll song "Cruising," Gene Vincent and The Blue Caps, 1956
Cruising with your lights on dim	Stupid, bughouse, not all there
Crumb crushers	Teeth
Crummy	Unpleasant, poor quality, worthless *"I sniff at the odour of rotting chow and* *tell Nick 'Crummy joint.'* *'Yeah,' Nick says, 'and crummy people.' "* From the novel *Killers Don't Care*, Rod Callahan, 1950
Crunchers	Feet
Cuban candles	Cigars

Cubistic	Square, straight, boring *"Mother, you can be such a drag sometimes, so utterly cubistic."* From the film *The Young Savages*, 1960
Cupcake	Term of endearment
Current concubine	Girlfriend, steady date
Cut out	Leave, depart
Cut some rug	Dance *Pioneer Chicago DJ Jack L. Cooper started a radio show in the early 1930s called "Rug Cutter's Special."* See the blues recording "Rug Cutter Swing," Henry Allen, 1934.
Cut the mustard	Get the job done See the country song "Too Old to Cut the Mustard," by The Carlisle Brothers, as performed by a teenage Buddy Holly onstage at his school in Lubbock, Texas in 1953, and dedicated to his teachers: *"Used to fight the girls off with a stick, now they say 'He makes me sick.' "*
Cut the scene	1. Stop making a fuss 2. Leave, depart
Cut up	Have a laugh, fool around
Cut up rough	Get tough, start a fight

D

D.O.A.	Dead on arrival, all washed up *" 'D.O.A.,' said the intern. 'It looks to me like a stiff dose of cyanide in a cocktail, probably a sidecar.' "* From the short story "Three Wives Too Many," Kenneth Fearing, 1956

Rudolph Maté directed a film noir called D.O.A. in 1950, from a novel by David Goodis (not to be confused with the 1978 documentary film of the Sex Pistols' U.S. tour).

Dabs   Fingerprints

Daddy-O   Term of address for a hipster
New Orleans DJ Vernon Winslow was broadcasting under the name Doctor Daddy-O in the late 1940s. He'd previously called himself Poppa Stoppa. Rock 'n' roll DJ Porky Chadwick of WAMO, Pittsburgh called himself "the Daddy-O of the radio, a porkulatin' platter-pushin' Poppa."

Billy Taylor put out a jazz recording in 1955 called "Daddy-O," and the phrase was also used as the title of one of the great late 1950s exploitation films.

Date bait   Boyfriend or girlfriend

Dame   Woman

Dancing on a dime   Dancing very close together
"Here at the ballroom young men and women come to dance rather than to listen. Preferably on a dime. To sock. In short, to rub bellies together and, thus, excite one another."
        From the autobiography *Talking to Myself,*
        Studs Terkel, 1977

"If you think I'm going dancin' on a dime your clock is ticking on the wrong time."
        Ella Mae Morse to Freddie Slack from the boogie-woogie recording "House of Blue Lights," 1946

Dangle   Leave, get lost, scram
"Outside, then. Take the air. Dangle."
        From the short story "Fly Paper,"
        Dashiell Hammett, 1920s

Dead man   Empty bottle

Dead on the vine   Worn out, exhausted

Dead on time	Hep, suave, in the know, on the beam
Dead presidents	Cash money, dollar bills
Dead soldiers	Empty bottles *"Get a load of them dead soldiers. Must have been some brawl last weekend."* From the film *The Devil Thumbs a Ride,* 1947
Deadfall	Nightclub or all-night restaurant that is really a clip joint
Deal around me	Leave me out of this, I'm not interested
Deep-sea diving	Oral sex *"He's a deep-sea diver* *with a stroke that can't go wrong,* *he's a deep-sea diver* *with a stroke that can't go wrong,* *he can touch the bottom* *and his wind holds out so long."* From "Empty Bed Blues Part 1," Bessie Smith, 1928
Deep six	Dispose of, kill
Delosis	"De-Lo-Sis—a young girl, pretty." From the booklet *The Jives of Doctor Hepcat,* Lavada Durst, 1953
Detroit disaster	Automobile
Deuce	Two dollars
Dice-joint	Gambling hall
Dick	Detective *"I'm just a square-toed dick. I can't match wits with you."* From the novel *The Clue of the Forgotten Murder,* Erle Stanley Gardner, 1934
Dig	1. Understand, comprehend, appreciate, approve of See the jazz recording "I Don't Dig You, Jack," Blue Lu Barker, 1939.

See also the jazz recording "I Dig You the Most,"
Kenny Clarke with The Ernie Wilkins Septet, 1955.
The flipside was called "Cute Tomato."
2. To notice, observe, or look around
*"I dug the square for Hassell; he wasn't there, he was
in Riker's Island, behind bars." i.e., I searched Times
Square for him, but he was in jail.*
From the novel *On the Road*, Jack Kerouac, 1957
3. General word used to punctuate a sentence, to
see if your audience is paying attention, dig?

Dig those mellow kicks	Enjoy yourself
Dime	Ten-year jail sentence
Dime dropper	Police informer—i.e., someone who drops a dime in the payphone to call up the cops.
Dime-grind palace	Cheap dancehall with girls available as paid dancing partners *"I work at the Palace Ballroom, But gee that palace is cheap . . . Ten cents a dance, pansies and rough guys, Tough guys who tear my gown."* From the jazz recording "Ten Cents a Dance," Ruth Etting, 1930
Ding dong daddy	A dude, a hepcat See the jazz recording "I'm a Ding Dong Daddy (from Dumas)," Louis Armstrong, 1930—also recorded by Slatz Randall and His Orchestra, 1930, and the country duo Zeb and Zeke, 1934. *Characters in Nelson Algren novels have a habit of singing this song, for instance in* Never Come Morning, *1941, and* The Man with the Golden Arm, *1959*
Dinner	Pretty young girl From the autobiography *Really the Blues*, Mezz Mezzrow and Bernard Wolfe, 1946
Dip your bill	Have a drink of booze

Dirty dozens   Trading insults back and forth, each one worse
than the last
" 'S'pose he tell you he was with you mama.'
'I don't play no dozens, boy,' Smitty
growled. 'You young punks don't know
how far to go with a man.' "
> From the novel *If He Hollers Let Him Go*,
> Chester Himes, 1945

"Ashes to ashes, sand to sand,
I like your mama but she got too many men . . ."
> From the blues recording "The Dirty Dozens,"
> Speckled Red, 1930

Dirty with money   Rolling in it, rich, wealthy

Disc   Record, platter, waxing, a solid slab of sound
In the late fifties, Mad *magazine did a parody of all
the current rock 'n' roll fan magazines and called it*
Diskville, *which claimed "Frankie Avalon's new
record is called* My Teenage Lips Are Chapped
from Kissing an Ice Cold Chick."

Dish   Good-looking person
"You're a swell dish. I think I'm gonna go for you."
> Jimmy Cagney in the film *The Public Enemy,* 1933

Dish it out   Hand something out: punishment,
information, etc.
> See the jazz recording "I Can Dish It, Can You Take
> It," Blue Scott and his Blue Boys, 1936.

Dish the dirt   Tell the story, give away secrets

Dissolve   Leave in a hurry, disappear

Dixie fried   Drunk
*Dixie, as well as being the traditional name for the
Southern states, is also one of the most popular
brands of beer in the region.*

"He hollered 'Rave on, children, I'm with ya,
Rave on, cats' he cried.

'It's almost dawn and the cops are gone
Let's all get dixie fried . . .' "
> From the rockabilly recording "Dixie Fried,"
> Carl Perkins, 1956

Do a Houdini Disappear, leave in a hurry

Do a number on someone Pull the wool over their eyes, deceive, con

Do right man Someone who plays it straight, who wouldn't cheat on their partner
> See the blues recording "Do Right Papa,"
> Butterbeans and Susie, 1925; the western swing
> recording "I'm a Do Right Papa," Leon's Lone Star
> Cowboys, 1935; the country recording "I'm a Do
> Right Cowboy," Tex Ritter, 1935.

Dog around 1. Nag, verbally abuse
"Give me a break, Papa,
don't throw your sweet mama down.
You've treated me so mean,
ain't you tired of doggin' me round?"
> From the blues recording "Give Me a Break Blues,"
> Ida Cox, 1927

> See also the blues recording "If You Don't Want Me
> (Stop Doggin' Me Round)," Jan Garber, 1924.

2. Following someone
"Who's the ugly lob at the end of the bar chilling us?
He's dogging me. Doesn't seem to care if I know it
or not."
> From the novel *Darling, It's Death,*
> Richard S. Prather, 1953

Doghouse Double bass
"The car radio gave me 'Whispers,' very softly, with
a lot of strings, a growling doghouse and a sobbing
trumpet."
> From the novel *Halo in Blood,*
> Howard Browne, 1946

Dogs	Feet
	"Keep your dog on it." i.e., *Keep your foot on the accelerator.*
	   From the novel *Red Harvest*,
	   Dashiell Hammett, 1929
	
	   See the blues recording "Got to Cool My Doggies Now," Mamie Smith and her Jazz Hounds, 1922

Doing it all	Serving a life sentence in jail
Doing next week's drinking too soon	Those extra shots of booze that you really don't need because you're totally plastered already
Doing the book	Serving a life sentence in jail " 'He told me to tell you not to worry about him.' 'He's doing the book, I worry plenty.' 'Well, he's a tough kid, maybe he'll get a break.' " From the film *The Killing*, 1956

Doll	Good-looking girl
	"It was a woman, a doll, a sensational tomato who looked as if she'd just turned twenty-one, but had obviously signalled for the turn a long time ago. She was tall, and lovely all over, maybe five-seven, and she wore a V-necked white blouse, as if she were the gal who'd invented cleavage just for fun."
	   From the novel *Always Leave 'Em Dying*,
	   Richard S. Prather, 1961

Dollface	Term of endearment
Domino	To stop, to finish
Don't get your gauge up.	Don't get excited, calm down.
Don't let the grass grow in your ears.	To be lazy or otherwise untogether

Don't let your mouth start something your head can't stand.	Shut up or I'll hit you.
Don't move a peg.	Stay still. *"When I say stop, don't move a peg . . ."* From the piano boogie recording "Pine Top's Boogie Woogie," Pine Top Smith, 1928
Don't raise no needless dust.	Don't make a fuss, don't go out of your way.
Don't strip your gears.	Be cool, don't blow your top.
Don't sweat it.	Don't worry about it.
Don't take any wooden nickels.	Be careful, watch your step. See the jazz recording " 'Tain't Good (Like a Nickel Made of Wood)," Jimmy Lunceford and his Orchestra, 1936.
Don't vip another vop.	Don't say another word.
Dope	1. Heroin 2. Information, e.g., *"What's the dope?"*
Dope it out	Reason things out, explain *"I tried to dope it out, a screwy thing like that. I added up and subtracted and tried to remember back to certain times and places, and all I got out of it was a headache."* From the novel *Savage Night*, Jim Thompson, 1953
Double-barrelled shotgun	Harmonica that can be played from both sides
Dough	Money *"Plenty tough boy, and rolling in dough. Always had a bankroll that would choke a mule."* From the novel *Little Men, Big World*, W. R. Burnett, 1951

See the jazz recording "What'll We Do for Dough?," Walter Anderson and his Golden Pheasant Hoodlums, 1927.

Doughnut	1. Automobile tire
	2. Blues slang for vagina
	See the blues recordings "Mama's Doughnut," Spark Plug Smith, 1933, and "Who Pumped the Wind in My Doughnut?," Washboard Sam, 1935.
Douse the Edisons.	1. Put the lights out.
	2. Close your eyes.
Douse the glim.	Put the lights out.
Down with the fish	Drunk
Drag	1. A bringdown, something depressing
	2. Influence, e.g., *"He's got a lot of drag with the politicians downtown."*
	3. "Fun, killer, swinger, dumb."
	From the booklet *The Jives of Doctor Hepcat*, Lavada Durst, 1953
	4. Dance
	"Nothing braces me up like a good drag across the slag with a hag . . ."
	Charming sentiments from the film *Shake, Rattle and Rock*, 1957
Drag-and-eat pad	Restaurant
Draggin'-wagon	A hot car, something really fast
	"He wanted to get out of the two-wheel class and own a draggin' wagon."
	From the novel *Go, Man, Go!*, Edward De Roo, 1959
Dragging your rear axle	Beating about the bush, prevaricating
	"Come to the point, you're dragging your rear axle in waltz-time."
	From the film *High School Confidential*, 1958

Dragnet	Major police search, city- or even countrywide " 'Are you throwing out a dragnet?' 'Sorry, no dragnet Charlie. We've got a book full of names, addresses and phone numbers to check.' " From the film *Side Street,* 1950
Drape	1. A suit of clothes 2. "To dress or to lounge." From the booklet *The Jives of Doctor Hepcat,* Lavada Durst, 1953
Draw a lot of water	To have a lot of influence
Draw one.	I'd like a coffee.
Draw one in the dark.	I'd like a black coffee.
Drift.	Get lost, go away, leave. " 'Beat it,' he said. 'Drift. Take the air. Scram. Push off.' " From the novel *The High Window,* Raymond Chandler, 1943
Drill	Shoot someone
Drilling	To walk, to move in a straight line
Drinking that mess	Tipping it back, sucking the bottle "Drinking that mess is pure delight, when they get drunk they start fighting all night." From the R&B recording "Drinkin' Wine Spo-Dee- O-Dee," Stick McGhee, 1949
Drinking the town dry	A wild night, hitting the bottle high
Drinking your lunch out of a bottle	Being an alcoholic

Driving	Having sex
	"I've been driving fourteen years,
	haven't had an accident yet . . ."
	From "Henry Ford Blues," Roosevelt Sykes, 1929
	See the blues recordings "Hard Driving Papa,"
	Bessie Smith, 1926, and "Hitch Me to Your Buggy,
	and Drive Me Like a Mule," Casey Bill Weldon,
	1927.
Drop that back into low and go by once more.	Can you say that again please.
Drop the veil.	Stop pretending and come clean.
	"Drop the veil, sister, I'm in the business myself."
	From the film *The Big Sleep*, 1946
Drugstore cowboy	Young loafer on the streetcorner
Drunk tank	Holding cell for prisoners brought in drunk
Dryer than a cork leg	Thirsty, in need of some booze
Duck soup	*In the writings of Dashiell Hammett this means a sure thing, something very easily accomplished. However, Nelson Algren uses it to mean something strange and not quite as it should be:*
	" 'I hope he knows what he's doin' is all,' Mama T. observed dubiously. 'It looked queer as duck soup to me.' "
	From the novel *Never Come Morning*,
	Nelson Algren, 1941
	For the Marx Brothers, it meant whatever the hell they wanted it to mean . . .
Dude	1. A suave cat, a hipster, well dressed
	The U.S. Phonograph Company issued a wax cylinder in the early 1890s by Russell Hunting called "Casey and the Dude in a Street Car."

Raoul Whitfield wrote a story called "Sal the Dude" for the October 1929 issue of Black Mask *magazine.*
2. Guy, man, fella

Duded up Well-dressed, sharp

Duds Clothes

Duked out Dressed up, well turned out
"He was all duked out in a hard-boiled collar and a blue serge suit. There was a hatchet-faced dame with him in a stiff black satin dress and a hat that looked like a lamp shade."
From the novel *Savage Night*, Jim Thompson, 1953

Dukes Fists
" 'You know how to handle your dukes, man,' he said. 'Shortest fight we've had around here yet.' "
From the short story "A Hood Is Born," Richard Deming, 1959

Dumb gat A gun fitted with a silencer

Dummy-up Fall silent, refuse to talk

Dump Dwelling, building, apartment. It can be in any condition from well preserved to falling down. The phrase "Nice dump you've got here" is intended as a compliment, not an insult.

Dungaree doll Hip girl wearing jeans
*"The flat top cats and the dungaree dolls
Are headed for the gym to the sock-hop ball,
The joint's really jumpin', the cats are going wild,
The music really sends me, I dig the crazy styles."*
From the rock 'n' roll recording "Ready Teddy," Little Richard, 1956

Dust 1. Kill
2. Leave, depart
"Get moving: we may have to dust, and dust fast!"
From the novel *The Fast Buck*, James Hadley Chase, 1952

Dustin' the keys	Playing piano
Dutch milk	Beer

E

The eagle flies on Friday.	Getting paid
Early bright	The early hours of the morning
Easy rider	Good at sex See the blues recording "I Wonder Where My Easy Rider's Gone," Tampa Red and his Hokum Jug Band, 1929. See also the blues recordings "Ride, Jockey, Ride," Trixie Smith and her Down Home Syncopators, 1924 (billed as "exciting enough to stir up a dead man"); "Rider Needs a Fast Horse," Ora Alexander, 1931; "Easy Ridin' Mama," Washboard Sam, 1937; and the vocal group recording "I'm Gonna Ride Tillie Tonight," The Fortunes, 1948.
Eat crow	Be humiliated, forced to apologize
Eat your mush and hush.	Shut up and eat your food.
Eats factory	Restaurant
Edisons	1. Eyes 2. Lights
Eggs in the dark	Eggs fried on both sides
Eighty-eight	Oldsmobile 88, a car from the early 1950s also known as a Rocket 88 *"Got me a date and I won't be late,* *Pick her up in my eighty-eight."* From the rock 'n' roll recording "Rip It Up," Little Richard, 1956

See also the rock 'n' roll recording "Rocket 88,"
Jackie Brenston and his Delta Cats, 1951.

Eighty-eights	Piano
Eighty-six	Ditch, dispose of, drop
Electric cure	The electric chair

*"Ned Beaumont smiled tepidly and asked with
mock admiration:
'Is there anything you haven't been through before?
Ever been given the electric cure?'"*
From the novel *The Glass Key,*
Dashiell Hammett, 1931

Elephant teeth	Piano keys

*"The cat that's pulling the elephant teeth is a
bonnet-flipper and makes a gang of mad beats."*
i.e., *He's a damned good piano player.*
From the booklet *The Jives of Doctor Hepcat,*
Lavada Durst, 1953

Elevated	Drunk, high
Embalmed	Drunk, loaded
Embalmer	Bootlegger
Embalming fluid	Alcohol
Empty enough to steal the dog's dinner	Hungry
Enamel	Skin

From the autobiography *Really the Blues,*
Mezz Mezzrow and Bernard Wolfe, 1946

Enough bread to burn a wet mule	Very rich

From the autobiography *I, Paid My Dues,*
Babs Gonzales, 1967

Equalizer	Gun
Eternal checkout	Death

Evaporate	Leave, depart, say good-bye
Evening rig	Formal dress, dinner jacket, black tie, etc.
Every-which-way drunk	Catatonic, totally plastered, drinking yourself insensible *"I was taken drunk that year—every-which-way drunk . . ."* From the short story "The Lost Decade," F. Scott Fitzgerald, 1939
Everything is much straight.	Things are fine, mellow, A-OK.
Everything plus	Good-looking, the works; e.g., *"She was a swell dame with everything plus."*
Executive session	Serious drinking *"I remembered the half bottle of scotch I had left and went into executive session with it."* Philip Marlowe in the short story "Trouble Is My Business," Raymond Chandler, 1939
Eyeballing	Looking at, observing *"For once no-one was looking at Trammell; all ten thousand or so were eyeballing me."* From the novel *Always Leave 'Em Dying,* Richard S. Prather, 1961

F

Face like the elevated railway	Ugly
Face like a Russian flag	Embarrassed
Fade out	Leave, often in a hurry
Fair shake	A decent chance, an equal opportunity

Fall down, juvenile	Stop bothering me, you irritating youth. From the film *Beat Girl,* 1960
Fall guy	One who takes the blame for something, sometimes an innocent party " 'They got me measured for the fall guy.' 'Now just a minute . . .' 'Sure, I'm the fortune hunter that hypnotised Marsha, who made her kill her father for his money.' " From the film *Touch of Evil,* 1959
Fall in	Arrive
Fall in and dig the happenings	Come on in and have a good time, listen to this
Fall out	1. Depart 2. Go to sleep
Fan	Pick someone's pocket
Fan someone's baggage	Search their belongings "I'm clean. Go ahead, fan me, c'mon . . ." From the film *Pickup on South Street,* 1953
Far out	1. Weird 2. Impressive
Feeling no pain	Drunk, high, loaded See the jazz recording "Feelin' No Pain," The Charleston Chasers, 1927.
Fess up	Speak up, give out some information, confess
Filling station	Bar or liquor store
Fin	Five-dollar bill
Fine as wine	Good, the best "They say it's fine as wine and really on the ball, No windows, no doors, it's just a hole in the wall." Amos Milburn describes his ideal nightclub, from

the boogie-woogie recording "Chicken Shack Boogie," 1946.

Fine frame, no parts lame   Good-looking, having a good figure

Fink   Informer, stool pigeon

Finger man   Someone who sets up another person, either for arrest or assassination—puts the finger on them
Raymond Chandler published a short story called "Finger Man" in the October 1934 issue of Black Mask *magazine.*

"They killed the Mover and they killed Anna, and they tried to kill me. They are now in bad trouble. I want the finger man. As soon as I figure out who he is, he's dead."
From the novel *Little Men, Big World*,
W. R. Burnett, 1951

"I picked up the guy in a flea-bag hotel on Doncelos—his doll fingered him—and picked up the swag with him."
From the novel *Darling, It's Death*,
Richard S. Prather, 1959

Fish   1. A sucker, a rube
2. A dollar

Fish wrapper   A newspaper

Fishtail   Movement of car where the rear end swings from side to side

Flake   Unreliable, no good, a waste of space

Flap your ears   Listen
"Go right ahead baby, my ears are flappin'."
From the novel *Your Deal, My Lovely*,
Peter Cheyney, 1941

Flash your welcome sign
Give me some encouragement
Your lips start me to burnin'
with a desire an' a yearnin',
to feel them cling to mine,
well if you're with me flash your welcome sign."
From "Are You with Me," Mel Robbins, 1956

Flat as a matzoh
Broke, out of cash

Flat on your can
Down on your luck

Flat tire
1. A letdown
2. Impotent
"Couple of lightweights . . . yeah, flat tires."
Joan Blondell talking about the men she's with,
who've both passed out from drink.
From the film *The Public Enemy,* 1933

Fleabag
Cheap rooming house or hotel

Flimflam
Deception, con, swindle

Flip
Go wild, get excited, real gone
"I flipped my lid
I blew my top,
When I got roarin'
On a real cool bop . . ."
From the rock 'n' roll recording "I Flipped,"
Gene Vincent and The Blue Caps, 1956

Flip your wig
1. Jump for joy, bust a gasket
2. Go insane, lose your cool
"I figured she was the type to flip good if she
flipped."
From the novel *Always Leave 'Em Dying,*
Richard S. Prather, 1961

Flippy
Really good, excellent, the most
" 'Doll, where have you been?'
'Right in your little heart, Doll.'
'You didn't say a thing about my outfit.'
'Flippy . . . real flippy.' "
Elvis charms his date, from the film
Jailhouse Rock, 1957.

Floating	Drunk
	"I poured her a slug that would have made me float over a wall."
	From the novel *Farewell, My Lovely,* Raymond Chandler, 1940
Floozie	Tart, dancehall doll, streetwalker
Floozie-joint	Whorehouse
Flophouse	Cheap rooms, doss house
Florida honeymoon	A dirty weekend, a holiday affair
Fly	Smart, sophisticated, in the know
	From the autobiography *Really the Blues,* Mezz Mezzrow and Bernard Wolfe, 1946
	In England in the early nineteenth century, the word was already in use as a term for someone who understood the latest slang.
	See the jazz recording "I Ain't Your Hen, Mr. Fly Rooster," Martha Copeland, 1928.
Fly it through to endsville.	Bring it to a conclusion.
Fly the coop.	Leave, often in a hurry; leave home.
Foam	Beer
Focus your audio.	Listen carefully.
Fogged	Killed, rubbed out
	"The smooth-faced young man had his pistol out again. 'I can fog him easy, Slats,' he said."
	From the novel *Red Gardenias,* Jonathan Latimer, 1939
Foggy	"Full, crowded, loaded."
	From the booklet *The Jives of Doctor Hepcat,* Lavada Durst, 1953

Folding green   Banknotes
*"Just put this hunk of the folding green back in your
saddlebag and forget you ever met me."*
> From the novel *The Little Sister*,
> Raymond Chandler, 1949

**For you and me
the chill is on.**   Our relationship is over.

Foul-up   A mistake

Four-flushing   Cheating, lying, untrustworthy
*". . . this goddam four-flushing town, all the
viciousness and cruelty." Horace McCoy praises good
old Hollywood, from the novel* I Should Have
Stayed Home, *1938.*
> See the blues recording "Four-Flushing Papa
> (You've Gotta Play Straight with Me)," Lillian
> Goodner and her Sawin' Trio, 1924.

A film called The Four Flusher *starring Marion
Nelson and George Lewis played the American
theater circuit in 1928.*

**Fracture your
toupee**   Go crazy

Fractured   1. Drunk
2. Real gone, blown away, excited
*"I'm fractured! fractured!
that music fractures me . . ."*
> From the rock 'n' roll recording "Fractured,"
> Bill Haley and The Comets, 1953

Frail   Dame, doll, sweetheart, main squeeze
*Eric Howard wrote a story called "The Fifty Grand
Frail" for the November 1938 issue of* Black Mask
magazine.
*"She was the roughest, toughest frail, but
Minnie had a heart as big as a whale."*
> From the jazz recording "Minnie the Moocher,"
> Cab Calloway and his Orchestra, 1931

See also *The Wailing Frail*, a late 1950s novel by Richard S. Prather.

Frantic threads Hip clothes, sharp apparel

Freak A fan of something, an enthusiast;
e.g., *a hot-rod freak*

Fresh fish special Bad prison haircut given to recent arrivals—the fresh fish
"What about your haircut? Do you want a good one or do you want a fresh fish special—they hack it up. A good one'll cost you three packets of cigarettes."
From the film *Jailhouse Rock*, 1957

Fried 1. Given the electric chair
2. Drunk or high on drugs

Fried, dyed, and swept to the side Having your hair done, the full treatment, having it straightened, colored, and set

Friend of boys on the loose Good-time girl, of the kind that frequently seems to show up in Mickey Spillane novels
"She was a taxi-dancer, a night club entertainer, friend of boys on the loose and anything else you can mention where sex is concerned."
From the novel *Kiss Me, Deadly*, 1953

Friends in the bank Money
"I've got a nice little joint at the Ambassador, with a built-in bar; I've got a swell bunch of telephone numbers and several thousand friends in the bank."
From the novel *Fast One*, Paul Cain, 1936

Frill Girl, dame—similar to frail
"Half the guys in Hollywood was tryin' to marry this frill . . . the other half already had."
From the novel *You Can Always Duck*,
Peter Cheyney, 1943

From soup to nuts Everything, the whole shooting match
Felix Arndt released a ragtime record in 1914 called "From Soup to Nuts."

Fronts	"Clothes, suits, money." From the booklet *The Jives of Doctor Hepcat,* Lavada Durst, 1953
Fruitcake	Crazy person, weirdo
Fumigate your brains	Smoke a cigarette
Funky	Smelly, obnoxious From the autobiography *Really the Blues,* Mezz Mezzrow and Bernard Wolfe, 1946 Kenna's Hall, a New Orleans jazz hangout on Perdido Street, which was Buddy Bolden's regular gig venue in 1900, was known to everyone as Funky Butt Hall, or F. B. Hall for short. See also "Ain't Love Grand (Don't Get Funky)," a jazz recording by John Hyman's Bayou Stompers, 1927. *In 1950s jazz circles the word was quite common, for instance "Funk Junction" by King Pleasure and The Quincy Jones Band, 1954, or "Creme de Funk" by Phil Woods and Gene Quill, 1957. That same year, the Gene Ammons' Allstars put out an album called* Funky.
Funnel	A heavy drinker
Fusebox	Head

G

G	One thousand dollars, a grand
G.I. Blues	Morbid fear of being in the army " '*He been reading in the paper where all the young men gonna be called to the Army,' Peaches said. 'He got the G.I. Blues.'* " From the novel *If He Hollers Let Him Go,* Chester Himes, 1945

See also the jazz recording "Desperate G.I. Blues,"
Cousin Jo with Pete Brown's Blue Blowers, 1946.

G-man   Government agent, the Feds, the FBI
> Dwight V. Babcock wrote a story for the January
> 1936 issue of *Black Mask* magazine called
> " 'G-Man' Chuck Thompson."

> See the jazz recording "G-Men," Cootie Williams
> and his Orchestra, 1941.

Gabber   Radio commentator or DJ

Gabfest   Argument, conversation

Gams   Legs
*When Mildred Pierce hits the headlines, a press
photographer yells at her in an effort to get a little
more leg in the picture: "The gams, the gams! Your
face ain't news."*
> From the novel *Mildred Pierce,*
> James M. Cain, 1943

Gargle   Drink

Gargle factory   Bar, alehouse

Gas   1. To talk
2. Something really good

Gasser   Something or someone that takes your
breath away
> From the autobiography *Really the Blues,*
> Mezz Mezzrow and Bernard Wolfe, 1946

*"I copped a gig at Mintons and one night Alfred
Lions came in to dig us. He said we gassed him, but
we were too far out for the people."*
> From the autobiography *I, Paid My Dues,*
> Babs Gonzales, 1967

> See the jazz recording "That's a Gasser,"
> Wingy Manone, 1945.

> " 'Hey gasser, you lookin' for me?'
> 'Fall down, juvenile . . .' "
>> From the film *Beat Girl*, 1960

Gassing the slobs Impressing your audience

Gassing your moss Getting your hair straightened

Gat Gun
"You know, you're the second guy I've met today that seems to think a gat in the hand means the world by the tail."
>> Humphrey Bogart in the film version of
>> *The Big Sleep*, 1946

Gate Hipster greeting for a fellow dude, short for "gate mouth"
>> In 1926 Columbia Records issued a record called "Gate Mouth" by The New Orleans Wanderers with an advert that read "Gate Mouth swings wide and handsome . . . this is the kind of mouth that stretches from ear to ear and buttons in the back."

Down Beat's Yearbook of Swing, 1939, *defined "gate" as a "word of greeting between musicians."*
>> See the jazz recording "Stomp It Out, Gate,"
>> Rosetta Howard and The Harlem Hamfats, 1938.

Gator In 1953, Doctor Hepcat wrote that the word "gator" was interchangeable with the word "cat."
*"The old jukebox was blowin' out the beat
The cats and the gators were shakin' their feet."*
>> From the rockabilly recording "Three Alley Cats,"
>> Roy Hall, 1955

Geek 1. Lowest type of carnival sideshow performer, often featured in a cage, biting the heads off live chickens
2. Awkward person, weird looking

Geets Money
>> See the vocal group recording "All My Geets Are Gone," The Five Blazes, 1947.

Gentle up a drink Add some more alcohol to the mixture,
make it more potent.

Germsville A hospital

Get a glow Get drunk

**Get both your
eyes wet** Get drunk

Get in the wind To leave

**Get my bread or I
take your head.** Babs Gonzales' time-honored phrase, designed
to persuade club owners to pay his band at the
end of the evening.
From the autobiography *I, Paid My Dues,* 1967

**Get off the fence,
Hortense.** Make a decision, say what you mean.

**Get out of your
fighting clothes
and come
to earth.** Don't take offense so easily, calm down.
From the novel *Little Caesar,* W. R. Burnett, 1929

**Get the blast put
on you** Getting shot, having someone drill you a
new navel
*"Occasionally someone got the blast put on him—
but only as a last resort."*
From the novel *Little Men, Big World,*
W. R. Burnett, 1951

Get wise Understand, learn something

Get with it 1. Be where it's at, make the scene, be aware
*"We're gonna have a downbeat
We're gonna have a ball,
Get 'em on their feet
Gonna rock 'em all,*

But we gotta get with it
'Fore the night is gone."
> From the rockabilly recording "Get With It,"
> Charlie Feathers, 1956

> See also the jazz recording "Git Wid It,"
> Paul Martell Orchestra, 1944.

2. Have sex
"Let's get with it, please baby . . ."
> From the novel *Go, Man, Go!*,
> Edward De Roo, 1959

Get your hambone boiled

Have sex
"I'm going to Washington
to get my hambone boiled,
'cause these men in Atlanta
bound to let my hambone spoil."
> From the blues recording "Nothin' But Blues,"
> Cleo Gibson and her Hot Three, 1929

Get your kicks

Have a wild time, become excited, enjoy yourself
"Get your kicks on Route 66."
> From the R&B recording "Route 66,"
> Roy Brown, 1946

Getting mighty crowded

Under pressure, tense

Getting the shakes

Becoming afraid, agitated, worked up

Gig

1. Musical engagement
2. Any job or occupation

Giggle water

Alcohol

Gimme some skin

Hipster handshake
> See the jazz recording "Give Me Some Skin,"
> Lionel Hampton and his Sextet, 1941.

"Now gimme some skin, and ooze it out . . ."
> From the film *The Wild One*, 1954

Gimp

Lame, someone who walks with a limp;
e.g., *Moe the Gimp, 1920s mobster who married singer Ruth Etting.*

Ginhead	A drunk, an alcoholic
Gin mill	Bar, saloon, taproom, speakeasy
	"One of the best Race releases is Okeh 8747, whereon the Hokum Boys discourse in haphazard and lighthearted fashion on the Folks Down South and the Gin Mill Blues . . ."
	From the magazine *Phonograph Monthly Review*, New York, February 1930
Gin mill cowboys	Bar regulars, bottle babies
Gin mill perfume	Alcohol breath
Gin palace	Bar
Give him a permanent wave	To send someone to the electric chair
Give him the air	Tell him good-bye, finish the relationship, ignore him
	"Dorothy Brock don't mean that to me. If it hadn't have been for me, she wouldn't have had a show to star in. She'd better not try to give me the air now."
	From the film *42nd Street*, 1933
Give him the heat	To shoot someone
	From the novel *Dames Don't Care*, Peter Cheyney, 1937
Give him the works.	Shoot him.
	"So you didn't try to make a deal before giving him the works?"
	From the film *The Maltese Falcon*, 1941
Give it the gas.	Step on it, get moving.
	"You can jump in my Ford and give her the gas, Pull out the throttle, don't give me no sass, Take your foot, slap it on the floor, When you get here we'll rock some more . . ."
	From the rock 'n' roll recording "End of the Road," Jerry Lee Lewis, 1956

"A detective jumps in my cab and says
'Follow that black sedan, it's full of thieves.' So I
give her the gas . . ."
From the film *Where the Sidewalk Ends*, 1950

Give it the go-by. Pass up the opportunity, decline.

Give me an intro Introduce me to this despicable person and I'll
to this snake and get the marijuana cigarettes for you to smoke.
I'll hitch up the From the film *High School Confidential*, 1958
reindeers for you.

Give out 1. Speak up, tell all, come across
2. Play music from the heart

Give the gate Send someone away, fire them, send them packing
"I wondered whether there wasn't some safe way of
getting Fay to give her the gate."
i.e., *Couldn't Fay find an excuse to sack her?*
From the novel *Savage Night*, Jim Thompson, 1953

Give the glad eye Leer at, flirt with, look over
" 'He doesn't look like a shamus,' he says. 'I've seen
him trying to toss Ava the glad eye. He acts more
like a hood on the loose.' "
From the novel *Killers Don't Care*,
Rod Callahan, 1950

Give the Telling someone to get here fast, get a move on
hurry call

Give the place Search the building
the broom

Glass or a How would you like your drink?
funnel?

Glasses *"She's a remarkable lady, she's seventy-four years*
old and she don't need glasses. She drinks right out
of the bottle, this cat . . ."
Dean Martin onstage at The Sands, Las Vegas,
February 1964

Glom	1. Acquire, obtain, steal *Dashiell Hammett in his novel* The Dain Curse, *1928, spells it slightly differently: "Looks like him* *and another guy glaumed the ice . . ."* 2. Observe, look at
Gobble pipe	Saxophone
Go, cat, go!	Exclamation of encouragement, hipster-style *"One for the money,* *two for the show,* *three to get ready* *now go, cat, go . . ."* From "Blue Suede Shoes," Carl Perkins, 1956 See also the novel *Go, Cat, Go!,* Edward de Roo, 1959.
Go home and wrastle with that one.	That's what I can do—see if you can do better.
Go into your dance, buddy.	Alright, let's hear it; speak your piece.
Go on a deep six holiday	To be buried, to die
Go pick yourself an orchid.	Get lost, scram.
Go press the bricks.	Take a walk, get lost.
Go the whole bundle	Take a chance
Go to a museum for your art lessons.	Stop leering at me.
God sure don't like ugly.	You get what's coming to you. From the autobiography *Really the Blues,* Mezz Mezzrow and Bernard Wolfe, 1946

"I don't tell nothin' but the truth, because God don't like ugly."
    From the novel *A Hearse of Another Colour*,
    M. E. Chaber, 1959

Going commercial   Becoming a prostitute, selling it on the street

Going rotary   Blowing your top, losing it, going wild

Going steady with Mary Jane   Having a marijuana habit

Going to fist city   Going to have a fight

Going to hell in a handbasket   Turning bad, going to waste, going down the tubes
    "Did that explain why I'm all mixed up? Why I'm a no-good bum . . . why I'm a delinquent slob going to hell in a handbasket?"
    From the novel *Savage Streets*,
    William P. McGivern, 1959

Going to slice city   Going to cut somebody up

Gold   Money

Gold digger   Someone looking for a rich partner
    From the novel *Gentlemen Prefer Blondes*,
    Anita Loos, 1926

    See also the film *Gold Diggers of 1933*, 1933.

Goldfish room   Police interrogation room, usually fitted with a one-way glass for observation purposes

Gone   Out of this world, superlative
    "I have found the gonest little girl in the world and I am going straight to the Lion's Den with her tonight."
    From the novel *On the Road*, Jack Kerouac, 1957

    "Gee Vince, when you sing, it's really Gonesville."
    Vince Everett (Elvis Presley) makes a big impression on a fan, from the film *Jailhouse Rock*, 1957.

Gone with the gin Drunk, out of it, plastered
See the jazz recording "Gone with the Gin,"
Hot Lips Page and his Band, 1940.

Good-gal Girlfriend
"My good-gal loves me,
everybody knows,
and she paid a hundred cash dollars,
just bought me a suit of clothes."
From the country recording "Blue Yodel No. 9,"
Jimmie Rodgers, 1930

Good sauce from the gravy bowl Alcohol
"We used to call booze 'sauce' and the gravy bowl
was a cup."
From the autobiography *Of Minnie the Moocher*
and Me, Cab Calloway, 1976

The goods Good-looking
"This dame is certainly the goods."
From the novel *Dames Don't Care,*
Peter Cheyney, 1937

Goo-goo eyes and wolf whistles Leering appreciation

Goof Mistake, error
Satirizing the writers of Playboy *magazine in the*
early 1960s, the Reverend Roy Larsen came up
with the following: "Give us this day our daily
Martinis—dry and smooth—and forgive us
our goofs, even as we overlook the goofs of
others . . ."

Goon from Saskatoon An idiot, a square

Gorilla Tough guy, mobster, strong-arm boy
"The two gorillas yank him to his feet and Merilli
slugs him again. This time hard in the guts."
From the novel *Killers Don't Care,*
Rod Callahan, 1950

Got it made in the shade.	It's done, taken care of; I've got what I wanted.
Gouge	1. Obtain *"I gouged twenty dollars out of her for expenses."* Philip Marlowe in the short story "Trouble Is My Business," Raymond Chandler, 1939 2. Swindle or cheat
Grab a flop.	Sit down, have a chair.
Grab some air.	Put your hands up, I have a gun.
Grabbers	Hands
Grandstanding	Showing off
Grape cat	Wino
Grass	Marijuana
Grasshopper	Marijuana smoker, weedhead
Graveyard shift	Night work

Gravy	1. Money
	"Maybe the Guardians wanted the gravy, or the glory, or maybe Trammell was just too damned stinking to live—but they knocked their boy off."
	    From the novel *Always Leave 'Em Dying,* Richard S. Prather, 1961
	2. Sexual fluids
	    See "You Can Dip Your Bread in My Gravy, but You Can't Have None of My Chops," a shy, retiring blues recording from 1925 by Virginia Liston. The previous year she released a song called "You've Got the Right Key, but the Wrong Keyhole."
	3. Something easy,
	e.g., *"It wasn't all gravy."*

Graze on some grass	Smoke the weed From the film *High School Confidential,* 1958

Grease	1. Protection money or a bribe
	2. Sexual fluids
	See the blues recordings "I Want Plenty Grease in My Frying Pan," Margaret Carter, 1926; "Fat Greasy Baby," Robert Peeples, 1930; "Take It Easy, Greasy," Lil Johnson, 1936.
Grease joint	Cheap restaurant
Grease monkey	Mechanic
Grease your chops	Eat
Greased	1. Killed
	2. Drunk
Greenbacks	Dollars
Greetings, gate, let's dissipate.	The proper salutation when meeting a fellow hepster at the bar, according to Cab Calloway's Swingformation Bureau.
Grift	A racket, swindle, or other illegal means of making a few bucks, not usually involving violence
Grifter	Cheap crook, swindler
	"By the time she was twenty-one in 1926, she definitely preferred Tenth Avenue to Fifth, grifters to bankers, and Hymie the Riveter to the Honourable Cecil Windown, who had asked her to marry him."
	From the short story "Fly Paper," Dashiell Hammett, 1920s
	Probably the most famous use of the word came in 1963, when Jim Thompson published his novel The Grifters.
Grind	Striptease performance
Grind house	Striptease joint, or cheap cinema

Grinding　　1. Slow, sexy dancing
"This is a real slow number playing, and one thing about China. She know how to do like a snake with them slow discs. I'm all for that, and we do some slow grinding."
> From the short story "The Rites of Death,"
> Hal Ellson, 1956

2. Having sex
In his 1957 novel A Walk on the Wild Side, *two of Nelson Algren's characters flirt with each other by discussing coffee grinding in a suggestive manner:*
" 'It's always best to grind your own, miss. For that way it's much fresher.'
'So you say. But what good is fresh if there ain't enough to satisfy? Mister, if you talkin' 'bout some little old scrawny-size pot I ain't interested. What I needs is a great big pot, enough for both morning and night.'
'So long as it make good cawfee, miss, size don't scarcely matter ...' "

"Bought me a coffee grinder, the best that I could find, bought me a coffee grinder, the best that I could find, Lord he can grind my coffee cause he has a brand new grind."
> From the blues recording "Empty Bed Blues
> Part 1," Bessie Smith, 1928

> See also the blues recordings "Ain't Got Nobody to
> Grind My Coffee," (b/w "Take Your Finger Off It"),
> Mary Stafford, 1926; "Organ Grinder Blues,"
> Victoria Spivey, 1928; "My Georgia Grind,"
> Lucille Bogan, 1930; "Steady Grindin',"
> James "Stump" Johnson, 1933.

Grinding mill　　1. Machine gun on tripod
"Tell him to set up his mill and start grinding."
> From the novel *Red Harvest*,
> Dashiell Hammett, 1929

2. Vagina

"She grinds my meal in the morning,
and she grinds it late at night,
she grinds it in a way
suit any man's appetite."
> From the blues recording "Grinding Mill,"
> Johnny Temple, 1939

Groan box Accordian

Groghound Drunkard, alcoholic

Groove a tune Cut a record, lay down some tracks, wax a platter
"We grooved a couple of tunes in New York and
caught a wire at a nitery here in Chicago."
i.e., We recorded a couple of songs and then got a
contract to broadcast from a nightclub.
> From the novel *The Lady in the Morgue*,
> Jonathan Latimer, 1936

Groover Someone righteous, hep, solid, on the square

Groovy *"Really good, in the groove, enjoyable."*
> From the autobiography *Really the Blues*,
> Mezz Mezzrow and Bernard Wolfe, 1946

" *'I decided at the last moment that I couldn't*
live without you.'
'You sound groovy . . .' "
> From the novel *If He Hollers Let Him Go*,
> Chester Himes, 1945

"It's the Calloway Boogie,
keeps you groovy
twenty-four hours a day."
> From the jazz recording "The Calloway Boogie,"
> Cab Calloway and his Orchestra, 1947

> See also the jazz recordings "Boy, It's Solid
> Groovy," Jimmy Smith and his Sepians, 1941, and
> "Groovy Like a Movie—Let's Get Groovy,"
> Bonnie Davis and The Piccadilly Pipers, 1944.
> (The B-side of the latter was called "I Don't Stand
> for That Jive.")

Ground smashers	Shoes or feet
Gumshoe	1. Detective, private eye 2. To creep around, to look for clues
Gunsel	Originally a term for a young person, punk, eventually it was used as a general word for a tough-guy or gunman *"Let's give them the gunsel. He actually did shoot Thursby and Jacobi, didn't he? Anyway, he's made to order for the part, look at him. Let's give him to them."* Humphrey Bogart giving Elisha Cook Jr. a hard time, from the film *The Maltese Falcon*, 1941
Gut-ripper	Knife, shiv *"Double-edged double-jointed springblade cuts-all genuine Filipino twisty-handled all-American gut-ripper."* From the short story collection *The Neon Wilderness*, Nelson Algren, 1947
Gut scraper	Violinist
Guzzle shop	Bar, speakeasy

H

Hack	Automobile
Hack-jockey	Taxi driver
Half a yard	Fifty dollars
Half-hipped	Not very enlightened or sophisticated From the autobiography *Really the Blues*, Mezz Mezzrow and Bernard Wolfe, 1946
Half-stiffed	Tipsy, under the influence

Hand in your dinner pail	Die *"He gives a big howl and hands in his dinner pail."* From the novel *Dames Don't Care*, Peter Cheyney, 1937
Hand it to them	Shooting at someone
Hand out a line	Lie, bullshit
Hang out your hearing flap.	Listen carefully.
Hangin' it in	Having sex (A phrase very popular with Jerry Lee Lewis.)
Hanging paper	Passing forged checks
Hanky-panky	1. Sex 2. A whore *"Helen wasn't no hanky-panky."* From the novel *Red Harvest*, Dashiell Hammett, 1929
Hard-boiled	Tough, streetwise *"I like smooth shiny girls, hard-boiled and loaded with sin."* Philip Marlowe in the novel *Farewell, My Lovely*, Raymond Chandler, 1940 *"My God! For a fat, middle-aged, hard-boiled pig-headed guy, you've got the vaguest way of doing things I ever heard of . . ."* Praise for the Continental Op, from the novel *Red Harvest*, Dashiell Hammett, 1929 *A record by Lee Barth called "Onie Gagen" was described by a reviewer in August 1930 as "a comedy monologue in hard-boiled, tough-guy manner."*
Harlem sunset	Bloodletting, knife wounds
Hash	Food

Hash-house	Cheap eating establishment, where standards are not exactly top-of-the-line

*" 'If it's that kind of job, I hoped you
picked a five-dollar house. You're too
young for the two-dollar trade, and personally
I wouldn't like sailors.'
'I'm a waitress in a hash-house.'
'It rhymes up the same way.' "*
> From the novel *Mildred Pierce*,
> James M. Cain, 1943

*"I'm sleeping in flophouses, eating in hash joints,
mooching for dimes."*
> From the novel *Murder on Monday*,
> Robert Patrick Wilmot, 1952

Hash-slinger	A cook, especially in a fast food joint

> See the jazz recording "Slingin' Hash,"
> Zoot Simms, 1950.

Hatchet man	Assassin, strong-arm guy
Have one on the city.	Drink some water.
Have yourself a time.	Go wild, push the boat out.
Having your teeth pulled	Being disarmed

*"I pulled his teeth, boss. He was carrying a .32 in
the shoulder holster."*
> From the novel *A Hearse of Another Colour*,
> M. E. Chaber, 1959

Hay	1. Marijuana 2. Bed

*"I was nuts about her then. Who wouldn't be? All
the boys were anxious to nudge her into the hay."*
> From the novel *Death Is Confidential*,
> Lawrence Lariar, 1959

Hay parlor	Bedroom

He ain't worth the powder it'd take to blow his nose.	I'm not impressed with him.
He could stand one more greasing, he's not slick enough.	He's not very impressive, a poor dresser or a poor performer.
He got it with the rats and mice.	He won it in a crap game. See the novel *The Dain Curse*, Dashiell Hammett, 1928.
He ought to have his wardrobe cleaned and burned.	He dresses like a square.
He'd put clothes on a fish.	He's a smooth talker, a con artist, the kind that would sell you Christmas cards in June.
He's just like the man in the casket—dead in there.	He's cool; he's a hepcat.
He's so sharp he's bleeding.	That is one well-dressed dude. From the autobiography *I, Paid My Dues*, Babs Gonzales, 1967
Head in a sling	Troubled, weighed down with worry
Head knock	The boss, the person in charge
Headache stick	Police baton
Headlights	Breasts
Headshrinker	Psychiatrist *Policeman: "Do you know if the boy ever talked to a psychiatrist?"* *Sal Mineo: "You mean a headshrinker?"* From the film *Rebel Without a Cause*, 1955

Heap	Automobile e.g., *"So I hopped in the heap and tooled it downtown."*
A heap of jack	Lots of money
Heaped to the gills	High on drugs

Heat	1. The law
	"Somebody called the heat
	They threw us all in jail.
	We had a lot of rhythm
	Nobody had their bail.
	The judge gave us a hearing,
	When he heard us play,
	He shouted for an encore
	In a real gone way,
	He hollered 'Wail, man, wail!' "
	      From the rockabilly recording "Wail, Man, Wail,"
	      Kip Tyler and The Flips, 1957
	2. Weapons

Heat-making gown	Low-cut dress

Heater	Gun
	"All right dad, shed the heater . . ."
	      From the short story "Goldfish," Raymond
	      Chandler, *Black Mask* magazine, June 1936

Heavy sugar	A large amount of money

Heebie-jeebies	Fear, apprehension, the shakes
	"Keep it up and you're going to have the heebie-jeebies for fair, a nervous breakdown."
	      From the novel *Red Harvest,*
	      Dashiell Hammett, 1929
	
	      See the jazz recording "Heebie Jeebies,"
	      Louis Armstrong's Hot Five, Feb. 1926.
	
	Ethel Waters released a blues called "Heebie Jeebies" in 1926, for which the Columbia Records adverts

read: "You all know the 'heebie jeebies.' Perhaps you've had them before. You just can't keep still . . ."

When B. B. King was still a DJ in the early 1950s, he ran a radio show in Memphis called Heebie Jeebies.

Heel
A louse, a punk, a bum
"Which one of you heels scratched the guy at West Cimmaron last night?"
> From the short story "Finger Man," Raymond Chandler, *Black Mask* magazine, October 1934

Heel-beater
Dancer

Heel the joint
Leave without paying

Heeled
Packing a gun

Heist
A robbery or theft

Hell-bent
Determined

Hen pen
Female prison

Hep
1. Hip, cool, righteous, in the know
"They said they were going to a real hep party, and that kind of party I'm still scared of, mister. I don't go to them." i.e., *a drug party.*
> From the novel *Violent Night*, Whit Harrison, 1952

" 'You're a thriller,' she told him. 'Where'd you get so hep?' "
> From the novel *Go, Man, Go!*, Edward De Roo, 1959

Mitchell's Jazz Kings released a song called "Hep" in 1922; Cab Calloway and his Orchestra made a jazz record called "(Hep Hep) The Jumping Jive" in 1939; and even Fred Astaire put out a record in 1940 called "Dig It (I Ain't Hep to That Step, But I'll Dig It), i.e., I haven't seen that dance before, but I'll soon get the hang of it.

2. To inform someone, to put them wise.
> The word was being used in this sense by street
> gangs in the early years of the twentieth century,
> as reported in the book *Apaches of New York* by
> A. H. Lewis, 1912.

> See the jazz recording "We the Cats Shall Hep Ya,"
> Cab Calloway and his Orchestra, 1944.

Hepcat One who is hep, totally uncubistic
*Down Beat's Yearbook of Swing, 1939, defined a
hepcat as "1. A swing devotee who is 'hep' or
alert to the most authoritative information, or
2. A swing musician."*

*Lavada Durst, a 1950s DJ with station KVET,
Austin, Texas, broadcast under the name of
Dr. Hepcat. He published a slang booklet in
1953 entitled* The Jives of Dr. Hepcat.

*Lawrence Lariar describes a nightclub on
Fifty-Second Street in New York in his 1959 novel*
Death Is Confidential: *"Hardly enough room to
swing a hep-cat in. The last time I counted the
tables, there were just two dozen. The take can't
be much for Ziggi, unless he's selling reefers on
the side."*
> See the jazz recording "Hep Cat Love Song,"
> Cab Calloway and his Orchestra, 1941.

Here's how. A toast when drinking

Here's your hat, what's your hurry? Get lost; go away.

Hey-hey 1. Sex
2. A disturbance, a fuss

Hi-pockets Nickname for a tall guy (The corresponding
nickname for someone short is Pee Wee.)
*In 1953, country music DJ Hi-Pockets Duncan from
KDAV, Lubbock, Texas, gave Buddy Holly his first
radio exposure, and briefly became the singer's first
manager.*

Hick	Country bumpkin, unsophisticated *"Whadda you hicks do around here for kicks?"* From the film *The Wild One*, 1954
Hide	A set of drums
High and fly and too wet to dry	Something, or someone, very good, pleasing
High-hat	Stuck up, putting on airs *"Look here gal don't you high-hat me* *I ain't forgot what you used to be* *When you didn't have nothin'* *That was plain to see,* *Don't get above your raisin'* *Stay down to earth with me."* From the bluegrass recording "Don't Get Above Your Raisin'," Lester Flatt, Earl Scruggs and The Foggy Mountain Boys, 1951
High roller	Ostentatious or heavy gambler
High sign	Signal, significant gesture, OK, warning *"One of his yegg men sat by the doors has seen me and has given his boss the high sign."* From the novel *Killers Don't Care*, Rod Callahan, 1950
High tone	Fashionable, expensive
High, wide, and handsome	Doing well, everything A-OK *"Jake married her after he left here and moved to New York—after he was riding high, wide and handsome. It must be quite a comedown for her, living like she has to now."* From the novel *Savage Night*, Jim Thompson, 1953 See the country recording "High, Wide and Handsome," Tex Ritter, 1935.
Hightail it	Run away, leave in a hurry
Himalayas	Chest *"Baby, you got the Himalayas knocked into a sombrero."*

From the novel *Grin and Dare It,* by Ricky Drayton, 1953, which continues in the following vein: "She had the kind of curves to make 3D seem flat; however drunk she got she could never have fallen flat on her face; she couldn't have stood against a wall without opening a window."

Hincty   Paranoid, nervous

Hip   In the know, worldly wise, clever, enlightened, sophisticated
See the jazz recordings "Hip! Hip!," Jack Stillman's Orioles, 1925; "Hip Chic," Duke Ellington and his Famous Orchestra, 1938; "Stop Pretending (So Hip You See)," Buddy Johnson and his Band, 1939; and the blues recording "You Done Got Hip," Roosevelt Sykes, 1942.

Hip to the tip   The pinnacle of hipness, a righteous dude

Hip your ship   To inform, to tell you something

Hipped   To understand, to possess knowledge, to be convinced of something
"You're still hipped on Medley as a killer? Hell, Frank, it doesn't make sense."
From the novel *The Lenient Beast,* Fredric Brown, 1957

Hipster   *"Someone who's in the know, grasps everything, is alert."*
From the autobiography *Really the Blues,* Mezz Mezzrow and Bernard Wolfe, 1946

"One who is well schooled in the hep world."
From the booklet *The Jives of Doctor Hepcat,* Lavada Durst, 1953

Hit   Underworld contract killing

Hit man   Assassin

Hit the bottle high	Get drunk *"Before you start hittin' that bottle over there, I want to do you a small favor, if you'll let me."* From the novel *The Man with the Golden Arm*, Nelson Algren, 1949 See the jazz recording "Hittin' the Bottle," Frankie Trumbauer, 1930.
Hit the bricks	1. Leave 2. Walk the streets
Hit the hay	1. Go to sleep *"Alright, precious, you'd better hit the hay. You sound all-in."* From the film *The Maltese Falcon*, 1941 2. Smoke marijuana
Hit the skids	To be down on your luck, busted and generally behind the eight ball
Hit the wall	To break out of prison
Hitched up	One-night stand *"I went out last night, an' I got hitched up . . ."* From the rockabilly recording "She Said," Hasil Adkins, 1964
Hittin' the hop	On drugs
Hittin' the jug	Serious drinking *"Well out to the dance hall And cut a little rug, Oh we're runnin' like wildfire, An' a hittin' that jug . . ."* From the rockabilly recording "We Wanna Boogie," Sonny Burgess and The Pacers, 1956
Hobo jungle	Tramp settlement or camp
Hoister	Pickpocket

Hold on to your chair and don't step on no snakes.	Listen up, get ready, brace yourself.
Holding	In possession of drugs
Holding down a package	Intoxicated, plastered, several drinks past the point of no return *"I was holding down a lovely package," comments Dashiell Hammett's Continental Op in a story from the 1920s called "The Golden Horseshoe."*
Holding on	Still sober; able to function *"Just remember the words of the great Joe E. Lewis. He said 'You're not drunk if you can lay on the floor without holdin' on.'"* Dean Martin onstage at The Sands, Las Vegas, February 1964
Hole in the wall	Low-class joint, cheap bar *"No windows, no doors,* *just a hole in the wall . . ."* From the boogie recording "Chicken Shack Boogie," Amos Milburn, 1946
Holed up	In hiding
Holler	Yell *"I wiggled and I hollered,* *Screamed and I cried,* *Don't shoot me baby,* *I'm too young to die . . ."* From the rockabilly recording "Don't Shoot Me Baby," Bill Bowen and The Rockets, 1956
Honey	Good-looking woman, a real doll
Honky tonk	Bar, juke joint, spit-and-sawdust club *"The honk-a-tonk last night was well attended by ball-heads, bachelors and leading citizens."* From *The Daily Ardmorite*, Ardmore, Oklahoma, February 24th, 1891, quoted by Nick Tosches in the *Blackwell Guide to Recorded Country Music*.

"I'm a honky tonk man,
and I can't seem to stop.
I love to give the girls a whirl
to the music of that old jukebox . . ."
> From the rockabilly recording "Honky Tonk Man,"
> Johnny Horton, 1956

The Emerson Military Band released the "Honky
Tonk Rag" in 1917, and Bennie Moten's Kansas City
Orchestra put out a jazz record in 1925 called
"Sister Honky Tonk."
> See also the country recordings "Honky Tonk
> Blues," Al Dexter, 1936 and "I'm Going to
> Get Me a Honky Tonky Baby," Buddy Jones,
> 1941.

Sophie Tucker starred in a film called Honky Tonk
for Warner Brothers in 1929.

Honky tonk angel   Good-time girl
"Let them honkytonkin' angels
be the girls I'll never love,
let 'em know it's you I'm cravin',
it's you I'm thinkin' of . . ."
> From the country recording "Let the Jukebox
> Keep on Playing," Carl Perkins, 1955

Honky-tonk hotel   A low-class flophouse
"It's funny, anyway. That girl had class, yet she was
living in that honky tonk hotel."
> From the novel *The Lady in the Morgue,*
> Jonathan Latimer, 1936

Hooch   Alcohol
"Keep away from bootleg hooch
When you're on a spree,
Take good care of yourself
You belong to me."
> From the jazz recording "Button Up Your
> Overcoat," Ruth Etting, 1929

Hooch hound   Drunkard

Hoochie-coocher   Striptease artist
"Folks now here's the story
bout Minnie the Moocher
she was a red-hot
hoochie-coocher."
From the jazz recording "Minnie the Moocher,"
Cab Calloway and his Orchestra, 1931

See also the blues recording "Hoochy Coochy
Blues," Lemuel Fowler, 1926.

Hood   Hoodlum, mobster, tough guy
"The crime climate had changed greatly since the
wild and lunatic Twenties. The big hoods were now
businessmen and owned hotels and summer resorts
and distilleries."
From the novel *Little Men, Big World,*
W. R. Burnett, 1951

See the jazz recording "March of the Hoodlums,"
Eddie Lang, 1930.

Hooey   Lies, rubbish

Hoof   1. Feet
2. Dance

Hoofery   Dance hall

Hoofing it   1. Walking
2. Dancing

Hooks   Hands, fingers

Hoosegow   Prison
"Trundle him off to the hoosegow—he'd look nice in
a pair of bracelets."
Waldo Lydecker in the film *Laura,* 1944

Hop   1. Drugs
2. A dance party
"You know I got my hot-rod down the shop
Gotta meet my baby at the Teen Town hop."
From the R&B jump recording "Teen Town Hop,"
The Philharmonics, 1958

See the jazz recording "Wednesday Night Hop,"
Andy Kirk and his "Twelve Clouds of Joy," 1937,
the same outfit who cut a tune called "What's Your
Story, Morning Glory?" in 1938.

See also the vocal group recording "At the Hop,"
Danny and The Juniors, 1957.

Hop in my kemp and take off for the casbah. "Get in my car and go to Lovers' Lane."
From the film *High School Confidential,* 1958

Hop joint Place where drugs are bought or smoked
"Went in the hop joint
smoking the pills,
in walked a sheriff from Jericho Hill . . ."
From the hillbilly boogie recording
"Cocaine Blues," Roy Hogshed, 1948

Hophead Drug addict
See the jazz recording "Hop Head," Duke Ellington
and The Washingtonians, 1927.

Hopped up 1. Intoxicated, drugged up
"You're a friend of mine, remember? You got the
brass down on you. A hopped-up hood tried to kill
you."
From the novel *Violent Night,*
Whit Harrison, 1952
2. Customized car
"Say, this baby really rolls along, is she hopped up?"
From the film *The Devil Thumbs a Ride,* 1947

Hopping a freight Hitching a ride on a freight train
" 'During the depression,' said the cowboy to me, 'I*
used to hop freights at least once a month. In those
days you'd see hundreds of men riding a
flatcar . . .' "
From the novel *On the Road,* Jack Kerouac, 1957

Horn 1. Trumpet
2. Telephone

Horse feathers   Rubbish, bullshit
                      See the jazz recording "Horse Feathers,"
                      Cliff Jackson and his Krazy Kats, 1930.

                      " 'We pretended to be struggling for
                      the gun. I fell over the carpet.'
                      'Ah, horse feathers!' "
                         Joel Cairo fails to convince the police,
                         from the film *The Maltese Falcon*, 1941

Hosed down   Riddled with bullets

Hot car   1. Fast car
                      2. Stolen car, one the police are looking for
                      "My Cad would be hotter than a strip-teaser's tassel
                      by now . . . "
                         Shell Scott realizes that the cops have a description
                         of his car, from the novel *Always Leave 'Em Dying*,
                         Richard S. Prather, 1961

Hot circle   A great record, a wild waxing, one of the platters
                      that matter

Hot in the zipper Sexually aroused, amorous

**The hot lead   Getting shot
treatment**

Hot little mouse Good-looking woman, a real gone chick
                      "He told me he was running around with a hot little
                      mouse named Leona Sandmark."
                         From the novel *Halo in Blood*,
                         Howard Browne, 1946

Hot man   A good jazz musician, capable of playing the
                      hippest music
                      There was a jazz band in the Storyville district of
                      New Orleans in 1910 called The Four Hot Hounds,
                      and Joe 'King' Oliver was one of the members.

Hot-pillow joint Cheap motel renting rooms by the hour

Hot-seat fodder   Criminal

Hot squat   The electric chair
> Erle Stanley Gardner wrote a story called
> "The Hot Squat" for the October 1931 issue of
> *Black Mask* magazine.

Hotcha   Expression of enjoyment in hipster circles,
popular in the twenties and thirties
> There was a venue in Harlem in 1932 called
> Club Hotcha.

Hotcha number   A good-looking woman

Hot rod   Fast or customized car
*"O'Brian got out of the car. He said 'You
ought to drive hot rods, Ed.'
I would. Except for my mother. She's
queen of the dirt tracks. She'd be jealous if
I muscled in.' "*
> From the novel *Violent Night,* Whit Harrison, 1952

*"Dig that crazy driver,
yeah dig that fool a hole.
Dig it down by the side of the road,
he can hear them hot rods roll . . ."*
> From the rockabilly recording "Dig That Crazy
> Driver," William Pennix, 1956

Hotsy-totsy   Fine and dandy, really good
*The word "hotsy" was originally a slang term for
a prostitute.*

*Prolific jazz bandleader Irving Mills ran an outfit in
the late twenties called Irving Mills and His Hotsy
Totsy Gang.*
> See the jazz recording "Everything Is Hotsy Totsy
> Now," The California Ramblers, 1925.

**Hotter than a
two-dollar pistol**   Sought-after, in demand, whether for reasons of
popularity or because you're wanted by the police
*"I was dead broke, on the lam, and as hot as a
two-dollar pistol with the authorities everywhere."*
> From the autobiography *Rap Sheet,*
> Blackie Audett, 1955

Hot-wire	To start a car without the use of keys
House hop	Rent party, a dance in someone's apartment
House peeper	Hotel detective
How come you do me like you do?	Why do you treat me this way? See the jazz recording "How Come You Do Me Like You Do?," Rudy Vallee, 1930.
How do you like them apples?	How does that grab you? What do you think of that?
How's the grouch bag holding?	Do you have any money on you?
Hum Dum Dinger from Dingersville	Beautiful girl, a total knockout See the country recordings "She's a Hum Dum Dinger," Buddy Jones, 1941, and "She's a Hum Ding Mama," Jack Hilliard and Leslie Palmer, 1938.
Hung up	1. Worried, anxious 2. Fascinated
Hungry	*"I'm so hungry I could eat the raw right stump of General Sherman."* From the novel *Kiss Tomorrow Goodbye*, Horace McCoy, 1949
Hunky-dory	OK, in order, fine *"There was I talking to myself,* *Feeling hunky-dory,* *A pretty girl passed by,* *I tried to catch her eye,* *She seemed to sigh* *'Hey, what's his story?' "* From the jazz recording "What's His Story," Harry "The Hipster" Gibson, 1946 *The Columbia Orchestra released a record called "Hunky Dory" in 1901.*
Hush house	Speakeasy, illegal gin-joint

Hush-hush	Secret
Hymn-hustler	Priest, sky pilot, bible-basher

I

I ain't comin' on that tab.	I don't agree with you.
I ain't saying you're wrong, but I ain't saying you're right either.	Diplomacy, the Jim Thompson way, from the novel *Pop. 1280*, 1964
I am cable and able to wake you.	I'm about to let you know what's happening.
I dig your lick.	I understand what you're saying.
I don't go for that magoo.	Don't hand me that line; I'm not falling for that kind of talk.
I don't know beans.	I haven't a clue; your guess is as good as mine.
I don't mean maybe, baby.	That's right, I really mean it; that's what I want to do.
I don't sound you.	I don't understand you.
I feel like Death Valley.	I'm thirsty.
I get it, but I don't want it.	I hear what you're saying, but I don't like it.
I got a lot of room in my ears yet.	Keep talking, I'm listening.
I got your signal clear and cool.	I understand you perfectly. From the film *High School Confidential*, 1958

I have heard the wind blow before. You're bluffing, don't hand me that line.

I tried to carry a stuffed moose head through a revolving door. Somebody beat me up.
From the novel *The Bedroom Bolero*, Michael Avallone, 1963

I wanna jump your bones. I'd like to sleep with you.

Ice 1. Jewels
2. To kill someone

Iceberg act Playing it cool

Iceman Professional killer

Ickie "One who does not understand swing music."
From *Down Beat's Yearbook of Swing, 1939*

"One of the upper crust, big shot, bankers, money people."
From the booklet *The Jives of Doctor Hepcat*, Lavada Durst, 1953

I'd rather drink muddy water, and sleep in a hollow log. I'm not interested.
"*Rather drink muddy water, sleep in a hollow log, than to be in Atlanta treated like a dirty dog.*"
From the country recording "T for Texas (Blue Yodel No. 1)," Jimmie Rodgers, 1927

If I'm lyin', I'm flyin'. I'm telling the truth, I swear.

If she don't bake, she doesn't get dusted. If she doesn't pay, she doesn't get any narcotics.
From the film *High School Confidential*, 1958

If that don't turn you on, brother, you ain't got no switches.	That should impress you—if not, then you're probably dead already.
If that's good, then my feet are kippers.	I'm not impressed.
I'm fresh out of a chatterbox.	I don't have a machine gun.
I'm gonna tear your playhouse down.	You're in trouble, I'm going to make you pay, you'll be sorry.

*"I caught you out, runnin' round,
now I'm a-gonna tear your playhouse down."*
> From the rockabilly recording "Nothin' but a Nuthin," Jimmy Stewart and his Nighthawks, 1957

> See the blues recording "I'm Gonna Tear Your Playhouse Down," Hazel Myers, 1924.

In a bluesey groove	Depressed, low-down
In a heap	Completely drunk
In a pig's eye.	That's rubbish; I don't agree with you.
In dutch	In trouble with someone, in their bad books

*"We ain't never been in dutch
We don't browse around too much
Don't bother us, leave us alone
Anyway, we almost grown."*
> From the rock 'n' roll recording "Almost Grown," Chuck Berry, 1959

In like Flynn	A certainty, a sure thing, deriving from popular stories of Errol Flynn's success with women
In my book you're way upstairs.	I really like you, I'm impressed.

In the bag	Drunk
	"He had been drinking steadily since his return from
	the Arizona Club nearly twenty-four hours earlier
	and yet one who did not know him well could never
	have told from his speech, his walk, or his visible
	reflexes that he was in the bag."

From the novel of the screenplay of *Ocean's Eleven*,
George Clayton Johnson and Jack Golden Russell,
1960

In the grip of the grape   Drunk

In the groove   Just right, solid, A-OK, righteous
Defined in Down Beat's Year Book of Swing, 1939,
as "1. Playing genuine swing, and 2. Carried away
by the music"

"She's in the groove, right on the ball
she's reet, petite and gone . . ."

From the R&B jump jive recording "Reet, Petite
and Gone," Louis Jordan and The Tympany Five,
1947

In there   Groovy, fine as wine, hip
"Now I'd say this chick is really in there . . ."

From the jazz recording "The Hipster's Blues,
Opus 7," Harry "The Hipster" Gibson, 1944

Indoor aviator   Elevator attendant

Interviewing your brains   Thinking

Iron   1. Kill
e.g., *"To iron someone out."*
2. Gun
" 'I'm keeping your gun,' Rudy went on. 'I'm taking
any iron that Carol has when she shows.' "

From the novel *The Getaway,* Jim Thompson, 1958

Iron bungalow   Prison

Iron men Dollars

" 'Hundred dollars,' I said. 'Iron men, fish, bucks to the number of one hundred . . .' "

> From the novel *Farewell, My Lovely*,
> Raymond Chandler, 1940

It 1. Sex appeal

Clara Bow, one of the most famous movie stars of the 1920s, had a huge success with a film called It. The sign on her grave at Forest Lawn cemetery reads "Hollywood's 'It' Girl."

> See the jazz recording "I've Got 'It,' But It Don't Do Me No Good," Helen Kane, 1930.

2. Sex organs

"You gotta wet it,
you gotta wet it,
dampen it so it can grow,
you gotta wet it,
you gotta wet it,
dampen it farmer you know,
sprinkle it and dampen it
and let the good work go on."

> From the boogie-woogie recording "Wet It,"
> Frankie "Half-Pint" Jaxon, 1937

"You didn't want it when you had it
so I got another man,
keep your hands off it,
it don't belong to you."

> From the blues recording "Take Your Hand Off It,"
> Lil Johnson, 1937

> See also the blues recordings "She Done Sold It Out," The Memphis Jug Band, 1934; "Try and Get It!," Bea Foote, 1938; and "I Want Every Bit of It," Bessie Smith, 1926

3. Virginity

> See the jazz recording "She Really Meant to Keep It," Johnny Messner and his Orchestra, c. 1940

It fits in with the beat. That suits the occasion; that's appropriate.

It fries my wig.	It blows my mind, I'm impressed, I'm astonished.
It looks like rain.	Someone is about to get arrested.
It turns my crank.	I like it, I approve, it turns me on.
It will pull you dead to the curb.	It'll knock you out, you'll love it.
It wound up in smoke.	It ended in gunfire.
It's a natural gas that you can't zig a zag.	You can't mend something that's broken; you can't fight City Hall; it's a hopeless case.
It's all right, I make it fresh every morning.	I'm paying the bill, don't worry, I've got plenty of money. From the film *Johnny O'Clock,* 1947
It's git-down time.	This is it, something's about to happen. *Git-down time is traditionally the time of the evening when prostitutes start work.*
I've got to take a rubdown in water.	I need a bath.
Ivories	1. Piano keys *"Here's a cat that lays a group of ivory talking trash and strictly putting down a gang of jive."* i.e., *He's a really good piano player.* From the booklet *The Jives of Doctor Hepcat,* Lavada Durst, 1953 *James P. Johnson, the blues, stride, and boogie pianist was billed as "King of the Ivories" when appearing at the New Star Casino in New York in February 1922.* 2. Teeth
Ixnay	No (pig latin for "nix")
Izzatso?	Really, you don't say? ("Is that so?")

J

J.D. Juvenile delinquent
"The rock 'n' rollers, the Twisters, the hipsters, the teenage J.D.s, all inside with their black leather, black denim, black hair, black eyes and black hearts."
  From the novel *Twilight Girls*, Judson Grey, 1962

Jack 1. Money
"The place is lousy with jack . . ."
i.e., *There's lots of money at that nightclub we're going to rob.*
  From the novel *Little Caesar*, W. R. Burnett, 1929

"All the jack he'd made in the rackets was gone. The state had latched on to part of it and the federal government had taken another big bite and lawyers had eaten up the rest."
  From the novel *Savage Night*, Jim Thompson, 1953
2. All-purpose term of address between hipsters, sometimes lengthened to "Jackson"

Jacket 1. A prisoner's file, both positive and negative, kept throughout the duration of their sentence
2. The sentence for a particular crime
"He'd been in short pants in the days when Louie Fomorowski was beating two murder raps. They'd gotten a one-to-life jacket on him for the second one, of which he'd served nine months in privileged circumstances."
  From the novel *The Man with the Golden Arm*, Nelson Algren, 1949

Jackrabbit blood Habitual prison escaper; said to have jackrabbit blood because of their continual tendency to run away

Jackroller Pickpocket, mugger, purse-snatcher

Jailbait   1. Underage girl
              See the novel *Jailbait*, William Bernard, 1951.
              2. Someone destined for prison
              " 'Are you interested in that?'
              'What's it to you?'
              'That's jail bait.'
              'He's just a kid.'
              'Yeah, that's what I said once. Maybe
              you'll be lucky. Maybe they won't send
              him back to prison. Maybe he'll get himself
              killed first.' "
              From the film *They Live by Night*, 1948

Jake   1. Correct, alright, in order, OK
              " 'Stick-up,' he said. 'Be very quiet and everything
              will be jake.' "
              From the novel *Farewell, My Lovely*,
              Raymond Chandler, 1940
              2. All-purpose term of address between hipsters
              See the R&B jump jive recording "Jake, What a
              Shake," Louis Jordan and The Tympany Five, 1939.
              3. Moonshine liquor

Jalopy   Automobile, not usually of the newest variety
              *"We got a ride from a couple of fellows—wranglers,
              teenagers, country boys in a put-together jalopy."*
              From the novel *On the Road*, Jack Kerouac, 1957

Jam-up   Something really good

Jane   Woman, girl
              *"You said he or she—do you think maybe it was a
              jane did the croaking?"*
              From the novel *The Corrupt Ones*,
              J. C. Barton, c. 1950

              *"I can't let you in just now. Ya see, I got a jane
              inside . . ."*
              From the film *The Public Enemy*, 1933

Jass   Jazz music, written both ways from 1913 up until
              around 1920, when the word "jazz" became the
              accepted spelling

*In New Orleans in the 1890s, there was a
snappily-titled proto-jazz outfit called The Razzy
Dazzy Spasm Band. Nick La Rocca's Original
Dixieland Jazz Band was formed in 1915, and they
put out the "Dixie Jass Band One-Step" in January
1917. In November 1917, they released "At the Jass
Band Ball," and by March 1918 it had become "At
the Jazz Band Ball." W. C. Handy put out a record
called "That Jazz Dance" in 1917, credited to
Handy's Orchestra of Memphis, while in June 1917
The Frisco Jazz Band put out a song called the
"Johnson 'Jass' Blues."*

Java   Coffee
"Gimme a shot of java, nix on the moo-juice."
i.e., *A cup of coffee, no milk.*
> From the autobiography *Really the Blues*,
> Mezz Mezzrow and Bernard Wolfe, 1946

> See the vocal group recording "Java Jive,"
> The Ink Spots, 1946.

Jazz   Having sex, or sexual fluids
*" 'Jesus!' she jeered. 'The nicest-looking guy I ever
saw and you turn out to be a lousy snooping copper.
How much? I don't jazz cops.' "*
> From the novel *The Killer Inside Me*,
> Jim Thompson, 1952

> See "The Jazz Me Blues," Lucille Hegamin, 1920; "I
> Want a Jazzy Kiss," Mamie Smith, 1921; and "I
> Wanna Jazz Some More," Kitty Brown, 1924.

Jazz baby   Jazz fan, usually a girl or flapper of the 1920s
> See the jazz recordings "Jazz Baby," Jim Europe's
> 369th Infantry 'Hell Fighters' Band, March 1919,
> and the "Jazz Babies Ball," Maceo Pinkard, 1920.

Jazz water   Bootleg alcohol
*John Joseph wrote a story called "Jazz Water—By
Special Delivery" for the May 1924 issue of* Black
Mask *magazine, which advertised it as "The
romance of the hooch."*

Jazzbo	Boyfriend
Jelly roll	Sex organs

"Jelly roll, jelly roll,
Laying on the fence,
If you don't try to get it
You ain't got no sense . . ."
> From "You've Got to Save That Thing,"
> Ora Alexander, 1931

> See the blues recordings "I Ain't Gonna Give
> Nobody None of This Jelly Roll," Dabney's Novelty
> Orchestra, 1919; "Nobody in Town Can Bake a
> Jelly Roll Like Mine," Bessie Smith, 1923; "Jelly
> Whippin' Blues," Tampa Red, 1928; "You'll Never
> Miss Your Jelly Till Your Jelly Roller's Gone," Lil
> Johnson, 1929; and the disarmingly modest "I Got
> the Best Jelly Roll in Town," Lonnie Johnson, 1930.

Jerks and fillies   Boys and girls, cats and kittens, studs and sisters
"Jerks and fillies" was DJ Gene Noble's all-purpose
name for callers to his show on WLAC Nashville in
the 1950s.

Jim   All purpose hipster term of address, usually
uncomplimentary

Jitterbug   1. Jazz dance
2. Someone who dances to jazz
Defined rather snottily by Down Beat's Yearbook of
Swing, 1939, as "a swing fan (not a true swing
music lover) who expresses his fondness for swing
music by eccentric dancing or emotional gestures
and gyrations."
> See the jazz recordings "Lullaby to a Jitterbug,"
> The Andrews Sisters, 1938, and "Jitterbugs Broke
> It Down," Ollie Shepard, 1940.

Jive   1. "v. To kid, to talk insincerely or without
meaning, to use an elaborate or misleading line.
n. Confusing doubletalk, pretentious conversation,
anything false or phony."
> From the autobiography *Really the Blues*,
> Mezz Mezzrow and Bernard Wolfe, 1946

Down Beat's Yearbook of Swing, 1939, defined the word merely as "the language of swing," however, they also list "jive artist" as "an elegant nothing, a ham who sells out."

Cab Calloway publicized his own booklets of jive slang with the recording "Jive (Page One of the Hepster's Dictionary)," Cab Calloway and his Orchestra, 1938, and Jiveformation Please, Cab Calloway and his Orchestra, 1938

The word shows up in numerous jazz and blues recordings, for instance: "Don't Jive Me," Louis Armstrong's Hot Five, 1928; "State Street Jive," Cow Cow Davenport and Ivy Smith, 1928; "Sweet Jivin' Mama," Blind Blake, 1929; "Jive Man Blues," Frankie 'Half-Pint' Jaxon, 1929; and the succinctly-titled "Jive," Duke Ellington and his Famous Orchestra, 1932.

> See also "Jive Bomber," recorded in London during the Blitz by Stephane Grappelli and His Quartet. Another jazz-related response to the Luftwaffe came in 1941 from Una Mae Carlisle with a song called "Blitzkrieg Baby (You Can't Bomb Me)."

Many rock 'n' roll DJs of the fifties used the name Doctor Jive, the most famous being Tommy Smalls of WWRL, New York City.

2. Marijuana
> See the jazz recording "Here Comes the Man with the Jive," Stuff Smith and his Onyx Club Boys, 1936

3. Insulting term of address, short for "jive-ass motherfucker"

Jive stick　A marijuana cigarette

Jive that makes it drip　Clouds that produce rain
> From the autobiography *Really the Blues*, Mezz Mezzrow and Bernard Wolfe, 1946

Joe below　"A musician who pays less than union scale."
> From *Down Beat's Yearbook of Swing, 1939*

John Hancock	Signature
Johnny-on-the-spot	Right place, right time e.g., *"Say the word and I'll be Johnny-on-the-spot."* (i.e., *I'm there when you need me.*) *"Friend you go out in a hall* *Want the joint to rock,* *All you do is give us a call* *We'll be Johnny-on-the-spot."* From the rock 'n' roll recording "Rockin' Is Our Bizness," The Treniers, 1956
Joint	Place, venue, establishment
Jolt	1. A shot of alcohol *"Sighing heavily I walked to the liquor cabinet* *and refilled my glass—this time with straight* *booze. I needed a good jolt and I planned on* *getting it."* From the novel *Two Timing Tart,* John Davidson, 1961 2. A shot of dope *"Once they get used to the jolts, they need four or* *five of them in a day. That'll cost anywhere from five* *dollars to ten dollars. I've found kids who spent their* *lunch money for dope."* From the novel *The Deadly Lover,* Robert O. Saber, 1951
Joy ride	Having sex
Judas hole	Small hole in the door of a speakeasy
Juice	Alcohol See the jazz recording "Buy Me Some Juice," Blue Lu Barker, with Danny Barker's Fly Cats, 1939.
Juiced	Drunk *"Let's drink some juice* *Let's all get loose . . ."* From the R&B recording "Juiced," Jackie Brenston and His Delta Cats, 1952

Juke joint	Cheap bar with dancing facilities
	*"Your nerves are jumping like a
	juke joint on Saturday night."*
	    From the novel *Halo in Blood*,
	    Howard Browne, 1946
	
	*"Well there's a little juke joint
	On the outskirts of town,
	Where the cats pick 'em up
	And they lay them down . . ."*
	    From the rock 'n' roll recording "Dance to the
	    Bop," Gene Vincent and The Blue Caps, 1957

Jump street	The beginning of something
Jumped up	Arrested, cornered by the police

Jumping	Wild, uninhibited
	*"Check your weapons at the door,
	Be sure to pay your quarter,
	Burn your leather on the floor,
	Grab anybody's daughter.
	The roof is rockin',
	The neighbours are knockin',
	We're all bums when the wagon comes
	I mean this joint is jumpin'."*
	    From the jazz recording "The Joint Is Jumpin',"
	    Fats Waller and His Rhythm, 1937

Jungled up	Living arrangements e.g., *"He's jungled up over in the Bronx"* i.e., *He's got a room somewhere in the Bronx.*
Just for kicks	For a laugh, for the hell of it

K

Keep plant.	Keep watch, act as lookout, stay in one place.
Keep your lamps on the prowl.	Keep a lookout; keep your eyes peeled.

Keep your nickel out of it.	Keep your opinions to yourself; stay out of this.
	"Keep your nickel out of this, wise guy."
	    From the novel *Red Gardenias*,
	    Jonathan Latimer, 1939

Kick	*"The kind of music you like, dance, cigarette or movie."*
	    From the booklet *The Jives of Doctor Hepcat*,
	    Lavada Durst, 1953

Kick off	To die, expire, bite the dust
	*" 'Another one kicked off on us, Captain.'
	'How many times do I have to tell you
	that a man can die in jail just the same as
	in hospital?' "*
	    From the novel *A Walk on the Wild Side*,
	    Nelson Algren, 1957

Kicking the gong around	Smoking opium
	    See the jazz recording "Kicking the Gong Around,"
	    Cab Calloway and his Orchestra, 1931.

Kicks	Thrills, excitement, a good time
	*" 'I don't like you when you're with them.'
	'Ah, it's all right, it's just kicks. We only
	live once. We're having a good time.' "*
	    From the novel *On the Road*, Jack Kerouac, 1957
	
	Meanwhile, back in the world of drugs, the soon-to-expire Mr. Birk is explaining his philosophy: " 'And you take it for kicks?' 'Kicks. Experience. Knowledge. Or sometimes, just plain old euphoria. You do dig euphoria, don't you?' he leered."
	    From the novel *The Icepick in Ollie Birk*,
	    Eunice Sudak, 1966

Kicksville	Something enjoyable, a blast, the state of getting your kicks
	"A voiceless roar issued from a half-dozen throats. The excitement of it, the thrill of it, spread through the group like wildfire. This was Kicksville! This was the utmost!"
	    From the novel *Run Tough, Run Hard*,
	    Carson Bingham, 1961

Killer-diller   A knockout, the best, something truly hep
*"Every band has a favorite killer-diller, which is sure
to be included on almost every program they
broadcast."*
> From Professor Cab Calloway's Swingformation
> Bureau, early 1940s

*" 'They call him Zand. He's a killer.' Joe and the
other boys laughed. Reisman eyed them steadily.
'How do you mean?' 'Sharpest dresser in town.
Poiple shoits! He'll moidah ya—ya bum!' "*
> From the novel *Little Men, Big World,*
> W. R. Burnett, 1951

> See the jazz recordings "Killer-Diller," Benny
> Goodman and his Orchestra, 1937, and "Killer-
> Diller," Gene Coy and his Killer-Dillers, 1948.

King bee   A stud, a ladykiller, top of the heap
*"I'm a king bee baby,
buzzin' round your hive.
I can make honey,
let me come inside . . ."*
> From the rockabilly recording "Got Love If You
> Want It," Warren Smith, 1957

King Kong   Moonshine, bootleg whiskey
*"On the second floor was a King Kong speakeasy,
where you could get yourself five-cent and ten-cent
shots of home-brewed corn."*
> From the autobiography *Really the Blues,*
> Mezz Mezzrow and Bernard Wolfe, 1946

Kisser   Mouth or lips
*"Chuck had the kisser of a clown, the wide-open,
honest, boyish smile of the natural buffoon."*
> From the novel *Death Is Confidential,*
> Lawrence Lariar, 1959

Kitten   Girl
"Where are you carrying the heater, kitten?"
> From the novel *Kiss Me, Deadly,*
> Mickey Spillane, 1953

Kitty	All-purpose term of address between hipsters
Knee pad	To beg
Knock a scarf	To eat
Knock a statue act.	Hold on, wait a minute.
Knock fowl soup	To die
Knock me a kiss.	Kiss me.
Knock over	Rob
Knock the polish off your toes	To dance *"Well my old gal's slow and easy,* *All the hepcats know.* *She gets that boppin' beat* *She knocks the polish off her toes."* From "Put Your Cat Clothes On," Carl Perkins, 1957
Knocked out	Drunk, intoxicated
Knockin' a jug	Getting drunk See the blues recording "Let's Knock a Jug," Frankie 'Half-Pint' Jaxon, 1929.
Know where the beat is	"To understand Swing." From *Down Beat's Yearbook of Swing, 1939*
Know your groceries	To be hip, aware, alert to the situation, to do things well, be accomplished *Peter Cheyney has a variant on this in his 1943 novel* You Can Always Duck: *"The guy who threw this Chez Clarence dump together knew his vegetables."*
Knowledge box	Head, brain
Knowledge box hitting on all cylinders	Intelligent, a smart customer

L

L7 A square, totally cubistic; A shape that can be made using both thumbs and both forefingers.

Lacquer crackers Records, platters, waxings, discs

Lam out of it Get lost, leave, go away
"Why the hell don't you lam out of here, bud? Before I throw a handful of fat coppers in your lap."
> From the novel *The Little Sister,*
> Raymond Chandler, 1949

Lame 1. Something bad, poor quality, disappointing
2. "Can't understand, dumb, not able."
> From the booklet *The Jives of Doctor Hepcat,*
> Lavada Durst, 1953

Lamping Looking or staring
"The customers were still lamping him and the doll like they were fillum stars. To one and all, such a drama could only have one end. Outsize Romeo rescues doll. Doll dates up. Nine months, she has a lil baby goil to match."
> From the novel *Crooked Coffins* by Griff, 1930s

Lamps Eyes
"I didn't think of anything but the blonde in my arms, and the .45 in my fist, and the twenty-six men outside, and the four shares of Consolidated I'd bought that afternoon, and the bet I'd made on the fight with One-Lamp Louie, and the defective brake-lining on my Olds, and the bottle of rye in the bottom drawer of my file cabinet back at Dudley Sledge, Investigations."
> Evan Hunter takes a sideswipe at Mickey Spillane's tough-guy style. From the short story "Kiss Me, Dudley," 1954

Latch on Become aware, understand

Late bright	Late in the evening
Later	1. Good-bye 2. A put down e.g., *"Later for that Lawrence Welk music, buddy."*
Lay it down	Speak your piece *"When he laid it, wham! it stayed there . . ."* From the spoken word performance *The Nazz*, Lord Buckley, 1951
Lay it on me.	Tell me, say what you've got to say; give it to me.
Lay some hot iron	Dance really well
Laying track	Lying
Layout	Living quarters, residence *"They lead us into Merilli's private apartment, which is a swanky layout."* From the novel *Killers Don't Care*, Rod Callahan, 1950
Lead poisoning	Getting shot
Leaky	Prone to tears " 'She's a little red around the eyes.' 'Oh, Christopher, a weeper. If there's anything I hate, it's a leaky dame.' " The wives get bitchy about a newcomer, from the film *Orchestra Wives*, 1942.
Let it hang.	Wait a minute, hold on.
Let me wake you, Jack.	Let me put you straight; let me tell you something.
Let's brush it hard and see where the dandruff falls.	Let's discuss this carefully. From the novel *Murderer's Row*, Donald Hamilton, 1962
Let's flat git it.	Let's get real gone; let's go wild.

Let's get out of the wheatfields, Mabel, we're going against the grain.	Dean Martin alfresco at The Sands, Las Vegas, February 1964
Let's keep the dead leaves off the lawn.	There's no use dragging up old arguments.
Let's tear.	Let's get in the car and drive fast.
Let's you and me nibble one.	Would you like a drink? From the novel *Farewell, My Lovely*, Raymond Chandler, 1940
Letting the air out of someone	Stabbing them
Lick	*"A hot phrase in rhythm."* From *Down Beat's Yearbook of Swing, 1939*
Lid	Head, brain e.g., *"Stash that idea in your lid, dad . . ."*
Lift the dogs	Pick your feet up, get a move on *"Lift the dogs, Janson . . . we ain't got all night."* From the novel *Chicago Chick*, Hank Janson, 1962
Like a rough night on the ocean	The worse for wear, bedraggled, not at your best *"He found himself feeling sorry for the broad. She really looked like a rough night on the ocean."* From the novel *Naked in Vegas*, John Denton, 1962
Line your flue	Eat From the autobiography *Really the Blues*, Mezz Mezzrow and Bernard Wolfe, 1946
Lip locking	Kissing
Liquid grocery	Store selling alcohol
Licorice stick	Clarinet

Living end

1. The best, superlative, righteous
2. The last straw, the limit
"Christ, he thought. This was the goddam living end. The kid in hot water again. Molly wise to Irene. He was sick and tired of the whole stinking rat race."
> From the novel *Run Tough, Run Hard*,
> Carson Bingham, 1961

Loaded

1. Drunk or full of drugs
" 'What's the matter with you anyhow?' 'He's just loaded, honey . . .' "
> From the film *Rebel Without a Cause*, 1955

2. Armed, packing a weapon, often written as "loaded for bear"
"Both of them had a bulge on the right hip that meant just one thing. They were loaded."
> From the novel *Kiss Me, Deadly*,
> Mickey Spillane, 1953

3. Rich, having plenty of money

Locoweed

Marijuana
"He was raised on locoweed, He's what you call a Swing halfbreed."
> From the boogie-woogie recording "Cow Cow Boogie," Ella Fitzgerald and The Ink Spots, 1946

Long bread

A large amount of money

Long gone daddy

In love, totally sent
"I'm a long gone daddy And I'm long gone for you."
> From the rockabilly recording "Long Gone Daddy," Pat Cupp and His Flying Saucers, 1956

Long good-bye

Death

Long green

A large amount of money

Longhairs

Highbrows, nonhipsters, squares, fans of straight music
> *Down Beat's Yearbook of Swing, 1939,* defines a longhair as "a symphony man, one who likes classical music."

Look like Tarzan, sing like Jane	Little Richard's recipe for rock 'n' roll success
Looker	A beautiful woman
Loose as a goose	Relaxed, at ease, intoxicated See the jazz recording "Loose Like a Goose," Bennie Moten's Kansas City Orchestra, 1929.
Loose brains	Stupidity
Loose wig	Open-minded, receptive to new ideas
Lounge lizard	Sharp-dressed dude with an easy line in patter
Louse up	Make a mistake
Louse machine	Limousine
Lousy	1. Something rotten, low class, no good 2. Full, replete, plentifully supplied *"The town's lousy with dames."* i.e., *There are lots of good-looking women here.* From the novel *The Dead Don't Care,* Jonathan Latimer, 1937
Lowdown	1. The full story, the inside dope 2. Feeling blue, depressed 3. Something treacherous or deceitful
Lower than a snake's belly	Depressed
Lower than the belly of a cockroach	Down, way down
Lubrication	Alcohol
Lug	Big guy, a heavyweight
Lunch hooks	Fingers

Lush	1. Alcoholic, heavy drinker

Lush   1. Alcoholic, heavy drinker
"Never saw this motherless lush in my life before, Captain. Ain't them blood stains on his jacket?"
> From the novel *The Man with the Golden Arm*, Nelson Algren, 1949

> For a suitably lurid pulp treatment of the evils of the demon booze, see the novel *The Lady Is a Lush*, Orrie Hitt, 1960.

> See the jazz recording "Nix on Those Lush Heads," Blue Lu Barker with Danny Barker's Fly Cats, 1939.

"You crummy, one-eyed lush!"
> From the film *They Live by Night*, 1948

2. Good-looking
"A lush little miss said 'Come in, please.'"
> From "Saturday Night Fish Fry," Louis Jordan and The Tympany Five, 1945

Lush dive   Cheap bar or gin joint

Lush hound   Drunkard

M

Main drag   Main street or thoroughfare
"I walked a couple blocks without sighting a bar, either on the main drag on the side streets."
> From the novel *Savage Night*, Jim Thompson, 1953

Main squeeze   Girlfriend

Main stem   Main street or thoroughfare
In Horace McCoy's 1937 novel No Pockets in a Shroud, *magazine editor Mike Dolan writes a regular column called "The Main Stem."*

Make   1. To see, to recognize
2. To seduce

Make a bulldog hug a hound	Very persuasive *"Big legged woman* *Keep your dresses down,* *You got somethin' baby* *Would make a bulldog hug a hound."* From the Jerry Lee Lewis recording "Big Legged Woman," 1958
Make like a fish	Have a bath
Make like a tree and leave.	Quit the scene, take off, vamoose. *"Well let's make like a tree and leave, let's make like a storm and blow,* *let's make like a chicken and fly this coop,* *let's make like a rock and roll . . ."* From the rockabilly recording "Make Like a Rock 'n' Roll," Don Woody, 1955
Make out like a foreign loan	To do well, be successful
Make the scene	1. To be there, to arrive or attend 2. To comprehend the situation, to dig something
Make with a mouthful of hi-fi	Sing me a song
Make with the feet.	Get moving, speed up, go away. *"On your way, dreamboat. Make with the feet."* From the novel *The Little Sister*, Raymond Chandler, 1949
Making time	Becoming acquainted, necking, getting off with someone *"Chuck would make time with any broad on my payroll. He's a young girl's dream, isn't he?"* From the novel *Death Is Confidential*, Lawrence Lariar, 1959

"We were making good time,
Getting in the know,
When the captain said
'Son, we gotta go'

I said 'That's alright,
You go right ahead,
I'm gonna Ubangi Stomp
Till I roll over dead.' "
> From the rockabilly recording "Ubangi Stomp,"
> Warren Smith, 1956

Man
1. All-purpose hipster form of address
2. A policeman
3. Drug connection or supplier

Marble city
Cemetery

Mark
A victim, a sucker

Maryjane
1. Marijuana, or a marijuana user
" *'You know what a maryjane is?*
You know what a mainliner is?'
'I think so. Are you trying to tell me
these boys are drugged?' "
> From the film *Touch of Evil*, 1959

2. Lesbian
" *'Your little Edie is a Mary Jane—a*
chicken for some dyke.'
'He means,' Stretch explained, 'a
les-bi-an. A girl that likes girls.' "
> From the novel *Twilight Girls*, Judson Grey, 1962

Maryjanes
Shoes
"My maryjane's been bitin' me for the past few
minutes . . . this one's bitin' my instep."
> Frank Sinatra onstage at The Sands,
> Las Vegas, 1966

Mash
Alcohol
e.g., *"Drinkin' mash and talkin' trash."*

Mash me a fin gate, so I can cop me a fry.
Lend me five dollars, I want to get my hair straightened.

Mashed
Drunk, blasted, out of your gourd

112

Mason-Dixon line   Anywhere out of bounds when necking,
smooching or parking and petting
> See the jazz recording "That's Her Mason-Dixon
> Line," Will Bradley and his Orchestra, 1941.

Match me   Give me a light
"Match me, Sidney . . ."
> Burt Lancaster to Tony Curtis, from the film
> *Sweet Smell of Success,* 1957

Mattress route   Sleeping your way to the top
*"Gloria Clarke had made the big time by way of the
mattress route. She was fruit for the newsmen,
always hot copy . . ."*
> From the novel *Death Is Confidential,*
> Lawrence Lariar, 1959

Max out   To serve your entire prison sentence,
with no parole

Mazuma   Money, the folding green

Meal ticket   1. Job
2. Sugar daddy or benefactor

Meat   Blues slang for penis
*"I'm going downtown
to old butcher Pete's,
cause I want a piece
of his good old meat . . ."*
> From the blues recording "Take It Easy, Greasy,"
> Lil Johnson, 1936

Meat show   Strip show, burlesque performance

Meat wagon   1. Police vehicle
2. Ambulance
3. Hearse
*"There's your customer, everything else is for the
meat wagon." Policeman to doctor after a shoot-out,
from the film* Side Street, *1950*

Memphis umbrella   A head full of serious hair grease or pomade,
generally water-resistant

113

Mess around
1. Have sex
2. Dance
"When I say git it,
want you all to mess around . . ."
From "Pine Top's Boogie Woogie,"
Pine Top Smith, 1928

See also the blues recordings "That Dance Called
Messin' Around," Sara Martin, 1926 and "Messin'
Around," Trixie Smith, 1926.

Mickey Finn
Knockout drug, usually disguised in an
alcoholic drink

Midnight ramble
Late-night show or dance popular in blues circles
during the 1920s.

Miseries
The blues, depression
"Sam, you sure do look like you've
got the miseries."
From the country recording "Lovesick Blues,"
Emmett Miller and his Georgia Crackers, 1928

"Gonna tell Aunt Mary 'bout Uncle John,
He claimed he had the miseries
But he's havin' lots of fun . . ."
From the rock 'n' roll recording "Long Tall Sally,"
Little Richard, 1956

Misery
1. Coffee
"They's a jernt on Market Street belongs to a guy
used to be a pal of mine in the field artillery. He'll
set us up to coffee an'. He's a Greek, an' his misery's
the hottest stuff in cups."
From the novel *Somebody in Boots,*
Nelson Algren, 1935
2. Gin

Mitt
Hand
"No, buddy. No you won't. Keep your mitts off
that desk."
From the novel *Red Gardenias,*
Jonathan Latimer, 1939

Mix it   To fight

Modernistic   With it, switched on, up to date
*See the jazz recording "You've Got to Be
Modernistic," Jimmy Johnson and Clarence
Wilson, 1930.*

Moll   Girlfriend, usually tied up with a gangster
*Erika Zastrow wrote a story called "A Moll and Her
Man" for the September 1928 issue of* Black Mask
*magazine, who billed it as "A Romance of the
Underworld."*

**Monday morning
quarterback**   Know-all, braggart

Moniker   Name

Mooch   1. An early jazz dance
*The Edison company issued a recording by Collins
and Harlan in 1914 called "Mootching Along,"
accompanied by the following explanation:*
*"For a long time, way back in the days before the
war, the negroes did a shuffling or lazy man's dance.
They could do it for hours at a time without tiring.
They called it The Mootch. The shuffle explains the
movement of the feet, and the 'mootch' defines the
lazy movement of the shoulders, and the sway and
rhythm of the body."*

*"Professor Charles H. and Mrs. Anderson will
present their latest ballroom dance* The Honolulu
Mooch, *Saturday October 15th, 1915."*
From an ad in the Harlem press, New York, 1915

See also the jazz recording "Shake It Up, Mooch It
Up," Eddie Heywood's Kansas City Blackbirds,
1927.
2. To beg
3. To swindle or cheat
*"Somebody said that Danny mooched Sam out of
something like a hundred thousand bucks."*
From the novel of the screenplay of

Ocean's Eleven, George Clayton Johnson and
Jack Golden Russell, 1960
4. To walk around aimlessly

Moocher Small time panhandler or beggar

Mooching the stem Begging on the street

Moo-juice Milk
From the autobiography *Really the Blues*,
Mezz Mezzrow and Bernard Wolfe, 1946

Moonshine Bootleg hooch, usually made out in the hills

Moonshiner One who makes bootleg hooch
*Early country star Fiddlin' John Carson, singer of
classics such as "Who Bit the Wart Off Grandma's
Nose" and "It's a Shame to Whip Your Wife on
Sunday," was described in a 1920s publicity handout
as a "moonshiner."*

Moose-eyes A leering dude

More dough than an army baker Lots of money

More fun than a hot transfusion Really wild, the best, a knockout
*"Well, crazy, you have just destroyed three thousand
of my corpuscles . . . Lady, you're more fun than a
hot transfusion, you're really plasma. I think we
could swing—if I knew the music."*
Shell Scott talks that talk.

From the novel *The Kubla Khan Caper*,
Richard S. Prather, 1966

Moss Hair

Most The best
*"She got a lot
Of what they call the most."*
From the rock 'n' roll recording "The Girl Can't
Help It," Little Richard, 1956

"Look, y'know, you could be the most, but all that old-style jive you got written up on the board is nowhere."

> Gang leader J.I. talking to the teacher. From the film *High School Confidential*, 1958

> See also the vocal group recording "She's the Most," The Five Keys, 1956

Most monster Mighty fine, the best

Moth's chance in a nudist colony Doomed, no chance at all

Mothbox Piano

Motivate your piechopper. Start talking.

Motormouth One who talks a lot

Mountain dew Bootleg liquor

Mouse 1. Black eye
2. Girl
" 'A mouse I've never seen before saves me from the cops and asks me to a conference in her motel room. Would I walk in cold?' She hesitated, and asked curiously, 'What's a mouse, Jim?'
'Don't act dumb. A mouse is a broad.' "
> From the novel *Murderer's Row,* Donald Hamilton, 1962

Mouthpiece Lawyer
" 'Polly, this is Morrie Tannenbaum, the famous criminal lawyer from Chicago . . .' 'Are you really a mouthpiece?' Polly demanded eagerly.' "
> From the novel *The Deadly Lover,* Robert O. Saber, 1951

Mouthwash Alcohol

117

Much beamy	Convivial, pleasant
Mudkicker	Prostitute, streetwalker
Muffin	Girl *"That muffin you grifted—she's OK. Stuck her chin way out for you."* From the film *Pickup on South Street*, 1953
Mug	1. Face, visage 2. A guy, a palooka, an ordinary Joe
Muggles	Marijuana
Mugshots	Photos in the police files of criminals' faces
Mugsnapper	Photographer
Mulligan stew	Cheap meal, poor man's food
Murderistic	Mighty fine See the jazz recording *"Murderistic,"* Jimmy Dorsey and His Orchestra, 1941.
Mush	Sloppy sentiment *"The world will pardon my mush but I have got a crush on you."* From the live recording "I've Got a Crush on You," Frank Sinatra, at The Sands, Las Vegas, 1966
Must have been tough on your mother, not having any children.	I don't know what you are, but you don't impress me.
Mutt	Dog
My finger's itching.	Keep quiet or I'll shoot you.
My meat, Jack.	That's right up my street, that's the one for me.

My solid pigeon, that drape is a killer-diller, an E-flat Dillinger, a bit of a fly thing all on one page.	How to compliment a young lady on her new and pretty dress, according to Cab Calloway's Swingformation Bureau
My tonsils are dry.	I'm thirsty, I could use a drink.

N

Nab	Arrest *"You nabbed his brother on a narcotics rap."* From the film *Touch of Evil*, 1959
Nabbers	Police, the forces of law
Naturally buzzin' cuzzin	A lively guy, a switched-on dude
Neck oil	Alcohol, booze
Necktie	The hangman's noose *"Well, they're gonna put a necktie on Gus he won't take off."* From the novel *Little Caesar*, W. R. Burnett, 1929
Necktie party	A lynching *"It sure looked as if I was about to be the guest of honor at a necktie party."* From the novel *Pop. 1280*, Jim Thompson, 1964
Nickel	Five-year jail sentence
Nickel-nurser	Stingy, a tightwad
Nickel rat	Cheap crook *" 'We've had twelve more legitimate citizen complaints against you this month, for assault and battery.'*

'From who? Hoods, dusters, mugs—a lot of nickel rats.' "
>> Hands-on police work by the men of the 16th Precinct, from the film *Where the Sidewalk Ends,* 1950

Night hawk
1. Taxi driver or cab
2. Late-night person
>> See the jazz recording "Night Hawk Blues," Coon-Sanders Original Night Hawk Orchestra, 1924.

>> See also the painting *Night Hawks,* Edward Hopper, 1942.

Nix
No, nothing, no thanks

No bats allowed.
"No ugly people invited (girls)."
>> Doctor Hepcat demonstrates his winning way with a party invitation. From the booklet *The Jives of Doctor Hepcat,* Lavada Durst, 1953

No soap.
No deal; nothing doing.

Noggin
Brain
" *'This dame,'* I note, *'has got a noggin that works.'* "
>> From the novel *Killers Don't Care,* Rod Callahan, 1950

No-goodnik from Creepville
A despicable person, a waste of space
After the word "beatnik" entered the language in the wake of the Russian Sputnik space mission, all kinds of slang words acquired similar endings.

"So the hell with Brett Sayers. Damn him to hell and gone. A no-goodnik from Creepville."
>> From the novel *Run Tough, Run Hard,* Carson Bingham, 1961

Noodle it out.
Think it through; come to a conclusion.

Nose candy
Cocaine
>> From the novel *Dames Don't Care,* Peter Cheyney, 1937. However, in the short story "Dead Yellow Women," Dashiell Hammett, 1920s, "nose candy" refers to heroin.

Nose paint	Alcohol

Not worth fifteen cents for parts	A loser, a nonentity, a worthless individual
	    "I don't get it, Ed. Billy-Billy isn't anybody. He
	    isn't worth fifteen cents for parts."
	    From the novel *The Mercenaires,*
	    Donald E. Westlake, 1960

Notch house	Brothel

Nothing shaking	No joy, nothing going on at all
	    "Why must she be
	    Such a doggone tease,
	    There's nothing shaking
	    But the leaves on the trees."
	        From the rock 'n' roll recording
	        "Nothing Shaking (But the Leaves on the Trees),"
	        Eddie Fontaine, 1956

Now that you've laid me out, when you gonna bury me?	Have you finished criticizing me, or do I have to listen to more?
Now you're getting yourself some oxygen.	Now you're talking, that's right.
Nowhere	A failure, something worthless e.g., *"Man, that lame Pat Boone platter they're* *spinning is strictly nowhere."*

Nuff sed	Need I say more; you can't argue with this.
	    At the Lincoln Theatre, Baltimore, in November
	    1920, The Four Jolly Jassers were billed as "a real
	    Creole Jass Band from the Land of Jazz, New
	    Orleans—Nuff Sed."

Numbers racket	Illegal lottery based on numbers printed in the
	financial or sports pages of newspapers
	    See the jazz recording "The Numbers Man,"
	    Jack Sneed and His Sneezers, 1938.

O

Off	To steal
Off the cob	Something corny
Oil merchant	A flatterer
On a roll	On a winning streak, lucky
On the beam	Intelligent, wise, alert

> See the jazz recording "Theme on the Beam,"
> Lem Davis, 1946

> "Well life is better
> if you're on the beam,
> and you dance to the rhythm
> of your wash machine . . ."
>> From the rockabilly recording "Wash
>> Machine Boogie," Bill Browning and
>> The Echo Valley Boys, 1956

> "I had bought her a container of coffee on the way
> uptown, a sop to my concern about her. I wanted
> her on the beam." i.e., I needed her to be thinking
> straight.
>> From the novel Death Is Confidential,
>> Lawrence Lariar, 1959

On the flypaper	Having your fingerprints on file
On the Jersey side	On the wrong side, in the wrong place
On the lam	On the run from the law
On the sleeve	Habitually injecting drugs

> " 'I been on the sleeve since I got out of the army,
> Doc,' Frankie told him."
>> From the novel The Man with the Golden Arm,
>> Nelson Algren, 1949

On the take	Corrupt, accepting bribes
One bad stud	A hard guy, an evil dude 　　See the vocal group recording "One Bad Stud," 　　The Honey Bears, 1954.
One-in-a-bar and live forever	A bass player 　　From *Down Beat's Yearbook of Swing, 1939*
One way ticket to Flipsville	Something mighty fine, really exciting
Onion ballad	A tearjerker, a sentimental song
Onion peeler	Switchblade knife
Only if you wanted to wear your face backwards for a while	Philip Marlowe tries to be reasonable, responding to a question with George Grosz's favorite tactic —a small yes and a big no 　　From the film version of *Farewell, My Lovely*, 1944, 　　with Dick Powell as Marlowe.
Orphan paper	Rubber checks, funny money, counterfeit currency
The other half of a half-wit	Stupid
Out on the roof	A night on the tiles *"I was out on the roof last night and I've got a hangover like seven Swedes."* 　　From the novel *The Lady in the Lake*, 　　Raymond Chandler, 1944
Out to the wide	Unconscious
Oversupply of mineral	Getting shot, being riddled with bullets *" 'The last guy who bought her a drink—* *they found him dead from an oversupply* *of mineral.'* *'Mineral?'* *He had too much lead in his body.' "* 　　From the novel *Red Gardenias*, 　　Jonathan Latimer, 1939

123

p

P.D.Q. Pretty damn quick
*"In the Holland box at the post office there's an
envelope with my scrawl. In that envelope there's a
parcel-room check for the bundle we got yesterday.
Now get that bundle and bring it here P.D.Q."*
> Philip Marlowe telling his secretary how
> to pick up the black bird, from the film
> *The Maltese Falcon,* 1941

Pack, shack, and stack All your belongings—your clothes, your home,
and your money

Pack your grip. Get your stuff together and go.

Packing iron Carrying a gun

Pad 1. Home, apartment, room
*"You gotta have a date with me before you fall in
my pad, darling . . ."*
> From the novel *If He Hollers Let Him Go,*
> Chester Himes, 1945
2. To tell, to inform

Pad money Rent money, as quoted in the street-gang study
Apaches of New York by A. H. Lewis, 1912

Pad your skull Absorb information, learn things

Painting the town Going out and having a wild night
*"A smile on my face
A song on my lips,
Pretending is all I do.
I'm painting the town red
To hide a heart that's blue."*
> From the jazz recording "I'm Painting the
> Town Red," Billie Holiday with Teddy Wilson
> and His Orchestra, 1935

"There ain't no use, hanging round,
While you paint up the town.
Crazy me, learnin' slow,
Baby you sure got your man feelin' low."
> From the country recording "Feelin' Low,"
> Ernie Chaffin, 1956

Palomino   Good-looking woman

Palooka   A mug, a punter, an ordinary joe
A disparaging term for a man, deriving from a
boxing term for a third-rate fighter.

Pan   Face
Hence the expression deadpan—showing as much
change of expression as a corpse might.

Panel joint   Whorehouse where the rooms have sliding panels
so that the clients can be robbed whilst otherwise
engaged
"A panel joint is a fast shuffling clip. The girl brings
the sucker in. A bedroom, see? They undress. She
puts the sucker's pants over a chair for him. While
they're in bed, a panel in the wall opens, and a guy
reaches in and frisks the sucker's pants."
> From the novel *Little Men, Big World*,
> W. R. Burnett, 1951

Panther piss   Bootleg liquor

Paper   A check

Paper hanging   Passing forged checks

Park the   Hide the stolen car.
hot boiler.

Park yourself.   Sit down.

Parking pet   Girlfriend

Parlor snake   Lounge lizard, smooth talker, oily customer
" 'Is that what the crowd does that keeps
following you around tonight?'

'What crowd,' she asked innocently.
'The fifty per cent of the sophomore class
that keeps following you around tonight?'
'A lot of parlor snakes,' she said ungratefully."
    From the short story "Josephine: A Woman
    with a Past," F. Scott Fitzgerald, 1930

Paws   Hands

Peach   Good-looking
"A peach, a plum, a reg'lar steamer!"
    From the novel *Night Club Moll,*
    Nick Baroni, 1930s

Pearl diver   Someone who washes dishes

Pedal extremities   Feet
    See the jazz recording "Your Feet's Too Big,"
    Fats Waller and His Rhythm, 1941.

Peel the ears and get it.   Listen closely.

Peeper   Private detective

Peg out   Die

Pegs   1. Legs
2. Trousers

Pen   Prison, penitentiary

Perforate   Shoot

Peter   A safe

Peterman   A safecracker

Picking iron out of your liver   Having gunshot wounds
" 'Keep on riding me, they're gonna be
picking iron out of your liver.'
'The cheaper the crook, the gaudier the
patter, huh?' "
    From the film *The Maltese Falcon,* 1941

Picking them up and putting them down	1. Running 2. Dancing
Pie chopper	Mouth
Piece of change	Some money
Pin	To observe, to notice
Pinched	Arrested
Pine box parole	To die in prison
Pineapple	Hand grenade or bomb *"Johnny stopped a pineapple."* i.e., *The dude's blown to pieces.* From the novel *Night Club Moll,* Nick Baroni, 1930s *"Look at this dump—four pineapples tossed at us in two days . . ."* From the film *The Public Enemy,* 1933 *Paul Cain wrote a story called "Pineapple" for the March 1936 issue of* Black Mask *magazine.*
Pipe	Saxophone
Pitch a bitch	Complain
Plant you now, dig you later.	Got to go now, see you later.
Planted	Buried *"If I need the stuff and don't have it, I'm dead. I'm not exaggerating. And if I get planted, you're sunk."* From the novel *Darling, It's Death,* Richard S. Prather, 1959
Plastered	Drunk, sluiced, oiled-up, loaded See the jazz recording "Plastered in Paris," Chauncey Morehouse and His Orchestra, 1938.

Platters   Records, discs, waxings
                  "The platters that matter . . ."
                            Defined as "a phonograph record" by *Down Beat's*
                            Yearbook of Swing, 1939

                  Black Mask magazine published a story set in the
                  record industry in May 1949 by Fergus Truslow
                  entitled "Pardon My Poison Platters."

Play bedwarmer   Sleep with someone

Play the chill   Ignore someone

Plumbers   Hit men, hired killers
                  "The big boys just give a couple of the plumbers
                  your address and that's it. If the first set of plumbers
                  don't fix the leak, they send another set."
                            From the novel *Little Men, Big World,*
                            W. R. Burnett, 1951

Plumbing   A trumpet

Poke in the snout   A punch in the nose

Poker pan   A straight face, expressionless

Pokey   Prison
               "The sheriff caught him out with Jezebel,
               Threw poor Okie in the county jail . . ."
                        From the rockabilly recording "Okie's in the
                        Pokey," Jimmy Patton, 1956

                        See also the jazz recording "Pokey Joe," Bob Skyles
                        and His Skyrockets, 1940.

Polluted   Drunk
                  " 'I've changed my mind'
                  'About what?'
                  'About getting crocked.'
                  'You mean you're going to get crocked?'
                  'Absolutely pie-eyed. Polluted. I'm going
                  to celebrate.' "
                        From the novel *This Is Murder,*
                        Erle Stanley Gardner, 1935

128

Pops	"A word of greeting between musicians." From *Down Beat's Yearbook of Swing*, 1939
Pouring on the coal	Stepping on the accelerator, driving fast
Pouring water on a drowning man	Cruel behavior *"I saw her one day with a big old pan,* *pouring ice cold water on a drowning man."* From the rockabilly recording "Evil Eve," Joe D. Gibson, 1957
Prayerbones	Knees
Preparing bait	Putting on makeup
Pressed stud	Well-dressed dude, a guy who's looking sharp
Pretzel	A French horn
Promote	1. Obtain, steal 2. Seduce *"That monkey's been trying to promote me for* *months."* From the novel *Red Gardenias*, Jonathan Latimer, 1939
Prowl car	Police vehicle *"He'd have called all the cops in all the counties, and* *there'd be even more prowl cars hunting me now."* From the novel *Always Leave 'Em Dying*, Richard S. Prather, 1961
Pruning your peach-fuzz	Shaving your face A phrase used by the rock 'n' roll DJ The Mad Daddy, who later had a song named after him on the album *Songs the Lord Taught Us*, The Cramps, 1980
Puff	"To ride, walk or fly." From the booklet *The Jives of Doctor Hepcat*, Lavada Durst, 1953

Puff down the stroll	Drive down the street
Pull a creep	Leave
Pull into the curb, Daddy-O, before your dreamboat becomes a battleship.	This relationship is doing you no good, give it up.
Pull up and squat.	Have a seat; sit yourself down. " 'Hi boys,' he said, and jerked a thumb to some chairs along the wall. 'Pull up and squat.' " From the novel *The Lenient Beast*, Fredric Brown, 1957
Pulling a judas	Putting the finger on someone, becoming an informer
Pulling the Dutch act	Committing suicide *"A girl pulled the Dutch act . . ."* From the novel *Vengeance Is Mine*, Mickey Spillane, 1951
Pump	Heart " *'What happened?'* *'Got him right through the pump with this.'* *'It's a Webley. English, isn't it?'* " From the film *The Maltese Falcon*, 1941
Punk	Cheap crook, loser, mug Philip Ketchum wrote a story for the January 1950 issue of *Black Mask* magazine called "One Sunk Punk."
Push-note	One-dollar bill
Pushed	Killed, assassinated, knocked off
Puss	Face *"Ludco's rat-like puss twisted into a grin."* From the novel *Night Club Moll*, Nick Baroni, 1930s

"My folks were tough. When I was born they took one look at this puss of mine and told me to get lost."
From the film *The Hitch-Hiker*, 1953

Put an egg on your shoe and beat it.
Go away, get lost.

Put on the feedbag
To eat
"Say, Daddy-O, do you know where a cat can have a ball and put on a fine feedbag?"
From the jazz recording "Two Blocks Down, Turn to the Left," Cab Calloway and his Orchestra, 1930s

Put some alcohol in the radiator.
Have a drink to warm yourself up.
"It's a cold night. Let's put some alcohol in the radiator."
From the novel *Savage Streets*, William P. McGivern, 1959

Put that in writing and I'll paste it in my scrapbook.
I don't believe you.
" 'I like you, Johnny O'Clock.'
'Put that in writing and I'll paste it in my scrapbook.'
'I mean it . . .' "
From the film *Johnny O'Clock*, 1947

Put the bite on someone
1. Blackmail, extort money
2. Borrow money

Put the polish on the furniture
Sort yourself out, reach the optimum level
"One little shot of bourbon to put the polish on the furniture."
From the novel *Your Deal, My Lovely*, Peter Cheyney, 1941

Put to bed with a shovel
1. Buried
2. Totally drunk

Putdown
Derogatory comment or criticism

131

Putting it down	Speaking, expressing an opinion

Putting it down Speaking, expressing an opinion
"I'm telling you what's being put down,
you better pick up on it . . ."
> From "Beware, Brother, Beware," Louis Jordan
> and The Tympany Five, 1946

"I'm putting it down, but you ain't picking it up."
> From *High School Confidential*, 1958

Putting on the dog Pretending to be better than you are,
putting on airs
" 'These three birds came in on the
Memphis train. Said they was with the
T.V.A., but I'd bet dollars to doughnuts
they wasn't.'
'What makes you think so?'
I don't know. They never looked right somehow.'
'Well, that's the world for you,' Sybil said
philosophically. 'People always putting on the dog,
trying to act like they're you-know-what on a stick.' "
> From the novel *Violent Saturday*, W. L. Heath, 1955

Putting on the style Dressing suavely, going upmarket,
having pretensions
"You were mine for just a while
Now you're putting on the style
And you've never once looked back
At your home across the tracks."
> From the country recording "Pick Me Up on Your
> Way Down," Charlie Walker, 1958

Putting up paper for yourself Bragging, singing your own praises
The reference is to running around town sticking up
posters with your own face on them.

Q

Q San Quentin prison
"She would be very nice to come home to after a
stretch in Q."
> From the novel of the screenplay of

Ocean's Eleven, George Clayton Johnson and
Jack Golden Russell, 1960

Q.T. 1. Secret
e.g., *"Strictly hush-hush, and on the Q.T."* i.e., *On
the quiet, just between you and me.*

"You understand this is to be strictly on the Q.T.?"
From the novel *The Glass Key*,
Dashiell Hammett, 1931

*"You thought your little romance
was on the strict Q.T.,
so if you want your freedom P.D.Q.,
divorce me C.O.D."*
From the country recording *"Divorce Me C.O.D.,"*
Merle Travis, 1946
2. "Cutie"—a slang term for a prostitute

Quail Woman, girl
*" 'I say, Professor, you've hunted in all
parts of the country. What kind of quail
is that there, over there by the tree?'
'That is very unusual, Doctor. That kind of
game is not typical in this section.'
'What would you say it was, Professor—a
red-billed roadrunner?'
'No, no, no, Doctor, why I could say with perfect
confidence that it's a black-topped cinch . . .' "*
Glen Miller's band gets frisky, from the film
Orchestra Wives, 1942

R

Rack 'em back.	Pull up the covers and go to sleep.
Racket	Criminal enterprise, scam, business
Ragtop	Convertible car
Railroaded	Framed, fitted up on false evidence

Raise sand	Make a fuss, create a stir *"You're always raising sand baby,* *and you're always doggin' me,* *I believe to my soul,* *you was stealin' back to your used-to-be."* From the blues recording *"Two-Timin' Woman,"* Casey Bill Weldon, 1936
Rap	Criminal charge
Rap sheet	Criminal record Blackie Audett, a bank robber who worked with Dillinger, Baby Face Nelson, and Capone, published an autobiography in 1955 called *Rap Sheet.*
Rat fink	A louse, a low-down dog *"I got the word for you* *Because that's what you is,* *You is a rat fink,* *You is a rat fink . . ."* From the rock 'n' roll recording "Rat Pfink a Boo Boo Theme," Ron Haydock and The Boppers, 1966
Rat someone out	Betray, sell someone down the river, inform on them
Rattler	Streetcar
Raw deal	Unfair break, tough shake of the dice *"Well I done had my last raw deal,* *Baby I'm through with you . . ."* From the rockabilly recording "Raw Deal," Junior Thompson and The Meteors, 1956
Read 'em and weep.	What do you think of that, I've won; I've beaten you.
Ready	Hep, alert, knowing, aware of the scene
Real gone	1. Far out, wild, uninhibited, totally sent

"Hold it fellas,
That don't move me,
Let's get real, real gone for a change . . ."

> The Hillbilly Cat puts 50,000 volts up the blues
> and winds up with rockabilly. From "Milk-Cow
> Blues Boogie," Elvis Presley, 1955

2. Insane

"You're a schizo, and real gone."

> Shell Scott receives some psychiatric advice,
> from the novel *Always Leave 'Em Dying*,
> Richard S. Prather, 1961

Real wild child Hip, gone, a righteous groover

"Well I'm just out of school
Like I'm real, real cool,
I've got to jump, got to jive,
Got the message I'm alive,
I'm a wild, I'm a wild one,
Ooh yeah I'm a wild one.
I'm gonna keep a shakin'
I'm gonna keep a movin' baby
Don't you cramp my style
I'm a real wild child."

> From the rock 'n' roll recording *Real Wild Child*,
> Jerry Lee Lewis, 1958 (Originally by Australian
> rocker Johnny O'Keefe, and later a sizable hit for
> Mr. James Osterberg.)

Red hot and ready to moan Fired up, all set for a wild night

Red onion Low drinking joint

> Louis Armstrong's first recording outfit when he
> left King Oliver's Band in 1924 was called The Red
> Onion Jazz Babies.

Reefer Weed, grass, dope

" 'Man, what's the matter with that cat there?'
'Must be full o' reefers.'
'Full o' reefers?'
'Yeah man.'
'You mean that cat's high?'
'Sailin' . . .' "

> From "Reefer Man," Cab Calloway, 1932

Harlan Lattimore and His Connie's Inn Orchestra
also recorded this tune in 1932, with "Chant of the
Weed" on the flipside.

Reet Right, OK
> See the jazz recording "Are You All Reet?,"
> Cab Calloway and his Orchestra, 1941.

Refrigerator Prison

Repo man Debt collector, someone who will come round and
repossess your car, your home, etc.

Rest the weight Sit down, take it easy
"Rest the weight, Bob, you must be tired of toting it
around all day . . ."
> From the novel *If He Hollers Let Him Go,*
> Chester Himes, 1945

Rewire job Medical attention
"They gotta doc here.
They're gonna rewire Crazy."
> From the film *The Wild One,* 1954

Rhino Money
"Give me my rhino instead of lip and I'll pull my
freight." i.e., *Give me my money instead of just*
talking and I'll be gone.
> From the short story "The Big Knockover,"
> Dashiell Hammett, 1920s

Ricky-tick Corny music, or anything clichéd

Riding academy Whorehouse

Riding for a fall In for trouble, taking chances

Riding herd Being in charge

Riding rubber Traveling by car

Riding the blinds	Hopping a freight, hitching a ride at the end of a baggage car on a train See I'm Ridin' The Blinds on a West-Bound Train," Frank Marvin, 1930.
Right guy	Trustworthy, dependable *"I came here with a straight proposition, take it or leave it, one right guy to another."* From the film *The Big Sleep*, 1946
Righteous	Cool, hip, in the groove, and generally suave as all hell
Righteous bush	Marijuana From the autobiography *Really the Blues*, Mezz Mezzrow and Bernard Wolfe, 1946
Ripe for the lilies	Dead
Roach	Marijuana cigarette, joint, reefer
Roach bender	Marijuana smoker
Roach killers	Shoes
Roadhouse	Lowdown roadside bar, outside city limits, often with a sleazy reputation *"They went further out on the highway to Buster's Roadhouse where chorus girls wore small panties. There were rooms to rent by the hour in the attached motel behind."* From the novel *Go, Man, Go!*, Edward De Roo, 1959 See the jazz recording "Roadhouse Blues," George Williams, 1926. (The flip was called "Bootlegging Daddy.")
Rock and roll	Sex See the blues recording "My Man Rocks Me (with One Steady Roll")," Trixie Smith, 1922.

"If you wanna satisfy my soul,
Come on and rock me with a steady roll."
> From the blues recording "You've Got to Save That Thing," Ora Alexander, 1931

"Want you to roll me baby,
Like a baker rolls his dough,
Reel and rock and roll me,
Baby all night long."
> From the blues recording "Rollin' Mama Blues," Ruby Glaze and Hot Shot Willie (Blind Willie McTell), 1931

"Gonna hold my baby as tight as I can,
Tonight she'll know I'm a mighty man . . ."
> From "Good Rocking Tonight," Roy Brown, 1946

> See also (among many others) the blues recordings "Rock, Jenny, Rock," The Georgia Strutters, 1926; "Rocking and Rolling," Robinson's Knights of Rest, 1930; "Rock It in Rhythm," Tampa Red, 1938; and "Rock and Rollin' Daddy," Merline Johnson, 1939.

Rock crusher Accordian

Rocket in your pocket Erection
"Let's go someplace
Where we can rock a bit
I got a rocket in my pocket
And the fuse is lit."
> From the rockabilly recording "I Got a Rocket in My Pocket," Jimmy Logsdon (a.k.a. Jimmy Lloyd), 1958

Rocks in your head Stupidity

Rod 1. Gun
"Turn around . . . then shed your rod. Drop it
on the floor."
> From the novel *The Fast Buck*, James Hadley Chase, 1952

2. Gunman

"Two of the hottest rods in town combing the joints looking for you and you don't even get bothered enough to stop eating."
> From the novel *Kiss Me, Deadly*,
> Mickey Spillane, 1953

3. Car, short for hot rod

Rod merchant — Gunman

Rodded — Armed, carrying a gun

Roll them bones — Roll the dice

"We're gonna pick 'em up an' shake 'em up
An' let 'em roll,
All night long we're gonna roll them bones . . ."
> From the rockabilly recording "Pick 'Em Up
> an' Shake 'Em Up," Cecil McCulloch and
> The Border Boys, 1956

Roll with the punches. — Go along with things; accept the inevitable.

Rooked — Cheated

Roost — Dwelling place, abode
> 1940s New York jazz venue The Royal Roost was
> also know as the Metropolitan Bopera House.

Roscoe — Handgun, firearm

"He propositions me we should heist the Jitney Jungle and I axes him where we can get a couple of rods, and he says we oney need one, Homer, and I got that, and he pull a roscoe off his hip."
> From the short story collection *The Neon
> Wilderness*, Nelson Algren, 1947

Rough-house — A fight or disturbance

Rubdown — A beating

Rub-joint — A cheap dancehall where dancing partners can be hired

Rubbed out Killed
" 'Five thousand bucks for rubbing out a horse.'
'OK, Pops, how do I get it?' "
From the film *The Killing*, 1956

Rubber Automotive transportation
"*You still on rubber?*" i.e., *Do you still have a car?*
From the novel *If He Hollers, Let Him Go*,
Chester Himes, 1945

Rubbernecker Tourist, out-of-towner gawking at the sights, or
anyone who stares
" 'I saw you giving Peter March the glad-eye.'
She said, 'You were rubbering at Carmel,
too . . .' "
From the novel *Red Gardenias*,
Jonathan Latimer, 1939

Rube A sucker, a hayseed, an easy mark

Rug 1. Hair
"*I've got to pick up on a barber because my rug
needs much dusting.*" i.e., *I need a good haircut.*
From the booklet *The Jives of Doctor Hepcat*,
Lavada Durst, 1953
2. Dance floor—as in *cutting some rug*

Rumble 1. Fight, especially a gang fight
2. A rumor, information
"*I'd like to know if it shows up. You're in a position
where you should catch the rumble, maybe, and if
you do, let me know fast.*"
From the novel *Darling, It's Death*,
Richard S. Prather, 1959

Run your mouth Talk a lot
See the jazz recording "You Run Your Mouth, I'll
Run My Business," Louis Armstrong, 1933.

Running around Being unfaithful, painting the town

Rupture head Idiot, someone who's lost it completely

S

Sack	Bed
Sacked out	Asleep
Sacktime	Bedtime
Sailin'	High on drugs
Same old same old	Habitual, the daily grind
San Quentin quail	Underage girl, the kind that can land you in prison Dale Clark wrote a story called "San Quentin Quail" for the October 1941 issue of *Black Mask* magazine.
Sap	1. Fool, fall guy e.g., *"Stop playing me for a sap."* 2. Blackjack

Satchel mouth	A wide mouth
	    Nickname for Louis "Satchmo" Armstrong.
	    See also the jazz recording "Satchel Mouth Baby," The Four Jumps of Jive, 1946

Saturday night special	Home-made or cheap handgun
Sauce	Alcohol, booze
Saucehound	Drunkard
Saucing a little on the much side	Getting drunk
Savvy	1. Knowledge, intelligence

"Jim Thompson was pure American writing at its best . . . He had more pistolero savvy than all the so-called great American writers."
> Harlan Ellison with some words of advice for college lecturers.

2. Do you understand me?

Sawbox   A cello

Sawbuck   Ten dollars
> See the jazz recording "(I Found a) Sawbuck," Johnny Crawford and His Orchestra, 1949.

Scarf   1. To eat
2. Food

Scat   1. Go away, get lost
" 'Shoo,' she said. 'Bon voyage. Scat. Scram. Good-bye. Yes?' "
> From the novel *The Icepick in Ollie Birk*, Eunice Sudak, 1966

2. Whiskey
3. Jazz singing using sounds instead of words
> A scat singer is defined by *Down Beat's Yearbook of Swing, 1939*, as a "vocalist who sings rhythmically, but without using accepted English words."

"Louis (Armstrong) first got me freed up from straight lyrics to try scatting . . . I don't know how it got started, really, the scat singing. I think one night in the Cotton Club I just forgot the words to a song and started to scat to keep the song going. It was 1931."
> Cab Calloway, from his autobiography *Of Minnie the Moocher and Me*, 1976. Cab recorded a jazz tune called "Scat Song" in 1932.

A fine example of scat being used in a song title would be the jazz recording "Wham (Re-Bop-Boom-Bam)" by Doctor Sausage and his Five Pork Chops, which was made available to a suitably appreciative public back in 1940.

Jazz singer Scatman Crothers, in the latter part of his career, provided one of the voices for the film The Aristocats, *before meeting a horrible end as a character in Stanley Kubrick's* The Shining.

Scatter gun	A sawed-off shotgun
Schmo from Kokomo	An idiot, a square
Scoff	Food
Scram	Leave in a hurry, blow the joint
The scramble egg treatment	Sex show

"*Ah yes, this joint I am familiar with. They do the scramble egg treatment on the floor to the delight of all onlookers.*"
> From the novel *Dig a Dead Doll*,
> G. G. Fickling, 1960

Scran	Food
Scratch	1. Kill someone 2. Money 3. To write
Scratched from the big race	To die
Scream sheet	Newspaper
Screaming mimis	Bad reaction to drugs, or withdrawal symptoms

> From the novel *The Screaming Mimi*,
> by Fredric Brown, 1956. Also filmed
> under the same title, 1958

Screw it on	Open up the throttle, cut loose
Screw up	Make a mistake
Screwed, blued, and tattooed	A wild night out

Selling a bill of goods	Swindling someone, lying, conning *"When we come around by the platform again I saw Socks and Rocky talking earnestly to Vic Lovell and Mary Hawley, Couple No. 71.* *'Looks like Socks is selling her a bill of goods,' Gloria said. 'That Hawley horse couldn't get in out of the rain.'"* From the novel *They Shoot Horses, Don't They?* by Horace McCoy, 1935
Send	1. To thrill, enrapture, and generally fry the wig *Down Beat's Yearbook of Swing, 1939*, rather narrowly defined it as "to arouse the emotions with Swing music." 2. To smoke marijuana
Seven come eleven	A dice player's expression calling for good luck See the jazz recording "Seven Come Eleven," Benny Goodman Sextet, 1939.
Sew up your mouth.	Shut up.
Sex appeal	Falsies
Shack up	1. Live with, cohabit *"Nothing could be finer* *than to shack up with a minor . . ."* Dean Martin, onstage at The Sands, Las Vegas, February 1964 2. To live somewhere *"Just so happens I know where he's shacked up."* From the film *Pickup on South Street*, 1953
Shag	1. "A form of dance inspired by Swing music . . ." From *Down Beat's Yearbook of Swing, 1939* 2. To tail or follow someone *"Mrs. Delancy is shagging a woman who was sitting next to Deirdre . . ."* From the novel *Murder on Monday*, Robert Patrick Wilmot, 1952

Shake a leg	Get moving
Shake a tail feather	A dance which involves waving your hind quarters around in what some guardians of youthful morals would take to be a shameless and lascivious fashion See the vocal group recording "Shake a Tail Feather," The Five Du-Tones, 1963.
Shake, rattle and roll	Having a wild time, originally specifically sexual A show called *Shake, Rattle and Roll* ran at the Lafayette Theatre in Harlem in 1927 "with a Cast of Fifty Noted Colored Entertainers." See also the jazz recording "Shake, Rattle and Roll," Charlie Barnet and His Orchestra, 1940.
Shake that thing	Dance *"When I say git it,* *I want you to shake that thing . . ."* From the boogie-woogie recording "Pine Top's Boogie Woogie," Pine Top Smith, 1928
Shake the lead out of your shorts.	Get moving; hurry up.
Shake till the meat comes off the bones.	Dance yourself ragged; strut your stuff.
Shake your business up and pour it.	Say what's on your mind.
Shake your feet.	Dance.
Shaking two nickels together	Broke, down on your luck *"I've been shaking two nickels together for a month,* *trying to get them to mate."* From the novel *The Big Sleep,* Raymond Chandler, 1939

Shakedown
1. Swindle, confidence trick, robbery, extortion
"But it'd serve that pokey right if somebody slapped him silly. He's been shaking down the greenhorns in here fourteen years."
> From the novel *The Man with the Golden Arm*, Nelson Algren, 1949

> See the jazz recording "Honey Don't You Shake Me Down," The New Orleans Jazz Band, 1924.

2. Police search

Shamus
Private detective

Sharp as a tack
1. Well-dressed, stylish
2. Intelligent, clued-up in the wig department
> See the jazz recording "Sharp as a Tack," Harry James & His Orchestra, 1941.

Sharp enough to shave
Well-dressed, stylish

She's my witch
She's my girlfriend.
"Artie swung to confront Rick. 'You better blow,' he said stiffly. He jerked a thumb at Pat. 'This is my witch.'
'Was, you mean,' Pat said loudly. 'I told you nobody orders me around.'"
> From the short story "A Hood Is Born," Richard Deming, 1959

"Got hair as black as night
Got a skirt that's ooh, so tight,
Tellin' you I've got an itch
She's my witch."
> From the rock 'n' roll recording "She's My Witch," Kip Tyler and The Flips, 1959

Sheik
Boyfriend

Shill
1. Someone in league with a cardsharp who helps to swindle other players by pretending to be an innocent participant in the game
"She's a shill for a gambler and she's got her hooks into a rich man's pup."
> From the short story "Trouble Is My Business,"

Raymond Chandler, published in *Dime Detective* magazine, August 1939
2. Police baton

Shimmy Shaking, suggestive dance, supposedly originated by the performer Little Egypt at the 1893 Chicago World's Fair
> See the jazz recording "I Wish I Could Shimmy Like My Sister Kate," The Cotton Pickers, 1922.

Shiv Small knife for stabbing people, sometimes homemade
> " 'Let's see the shiv,' he said.
> 'The what?'
> 'The pig-sticker, the switchblade, the knife, for Christ's sake. Don't you understand English?' "
> From the novel *Savage Night*, Jim Thompson, 1953

Shoo-in A certainty, bound to win

Shoot the sherbert to me, Herbert. Give me a shot of booze. Also, "Slip the juice to me, Bruce," and "Pour a gallon in me, Alan."

Shoot the works. Spill the beans; tell all.

Shoot your cookies Vomit
> "You better go lay down somewhere, buddy. If I'm any judge of color, you're goin' to shoot your cookies."
> From the short story "Finger Man," Raymond Chandler, 1934

Shooting a line Lying, telling a fanciful story

Short An automobile
> "Your fly chick is looking most frantic and your short is all gassed up and ready to roll."
> From the booklet *The Jives of Doctor Hepcat*, Lavada Durst, 1953

Short con Short-term confidence trick

Shot all to hell Worn out, broken, destroyed

147

Shot-rodder	Someone who's lost it, a crazy guy, a mess
Shove in your clutch.	Get moving; get on with it.
Shovel city	To like something, i.e., to dig it
Showcasing	Showing off, bragging
Shower down	Empty your pockets
Shroud-tailor	Undertaker
Shuck and jive	Mess around, waste time
Shucker	Stripper, burlesque dancer
Shutterbug	Photographer
Sidekick	Follower, pal, flunky
Sideman	Musician in a band, but not the leader of the band
Sides	Records
Sing	Confess, spill the beans
Sinhound	A priest
Sissy gun	Small-caliber weapon
Sister	Dame, doll, etc. *"She's a first-class four flushin' double dealin' twicin' sister of Satan who would take a sleepin' man for the gold stoppin' in his right-hand eye tooth."* From the novel *Dames Don't Care*, Peter Cheyney, 1937
Six-gun payoff	Death, getting shot *"You saw a nice way to drop it in my lap and promised the two witnesses a six-gun payoff unless they saw it your way."* From the novel *Vengeance Is Mine*, Mickey Spillane, 1951

Sixty minute man	Lover with staying power *"Looky here girls I'm telling you now they call me Lovin' Dan, I rock 'em, roll 'em all night long, I'm a sixty minute man . . ."* From the vocal group recording "Sixty Minute Man," Billy Ward and The Dominoes, 1950
Sizzler	The electric chair
Ski ride	Cocaine binge
Skin beater	Drummer
Skin show	Striptease performance
Skinny	Information, hot news
Skins	A kit of drums
Skull orchard	Cemetery
Skull work	Thinking
Sky pilot	Preacher
Slammer	Prison
Slap happy	Keen, possibly over-enthusiastic *"He's a slap-happy bird with a gun."* From the film *The Devil Thumbs a Ride*, 1947
Slaughter in the pan	Beefsteak
Slave	A job, employment
Slay me now, don't want to go another further.	I'm having a really good time.
Slinky piece of homework	Good-looking woman *"She's a slinky piece of homework with auburn hair*

and green eyes. She's wearing a low cut dress
of shimmering black which clings seductively to
her ripe curves. Me, I get a thrill just looking
at her."

> From the novel *Killers Don't Care*,
> Rod Callahan, 1950

Slip him the boodle Give him the money

Slip him the dose Shoot him

Slipped disc party A house hop with the wildest waxings

" 'You goin' to Norma's, Eliz? It's a slipped disc
party.'
'Will do, Mildew.'
I said 'I don't want to be an old square,
but what's a slipped disc party?'
'Discs are platters, you know, records, and
slipped means, well, you're out of this
world, slipped over the edge.' "

> From the novel *Drive East on 66*,
> Richard Wormser, 1962

Slop Food

Sloppy drunk Soused, smashed, juiced to the gills

> See the jazz recording "Sloppy Drunk Woman,"
> Blue Chip Norridge Mayhams and
> His Blue Boys, 1936.

"Drinkin' that mess is pure delight,
Get sloppy drunk and start fightin' all night . . ."

> From the R&B recording "Drinkin' Wine
> Spo-Dee-O-Dee," Stick McGhee, 1949

Slower than molasses in January Not very bright, not quick on the uptake

Slug 1. A bullet

" 'Shut up, you squealer!' Baird exclaimed. 'We're

both in this! *You try and walk out on me and I'll put a slug into you!'* "

> From the novel *The Fast Buck*,
> James Hadley Chase, 1952

2. A punch

" *'Orlik?' he sniffed, checking it against his memory. 'Not the big shot? Last time I read the name, he slugged a guy in a city club. Right?'* "

> From the novel *Death Is Confidential*,
> Lawrence Lariar, 1959

3. A dollar

4. A shot of booze

"She gets a few slugs under her girdle and she thinks it's Christmas."

> From the novel *Red Gardenias*,
> Jonathan Latimer, 1939

Slush pump	A trombone
A smack in the face with a steam shovel	A punch in the mouth
Smart up in the top storey	Intelligent
Smeller	Nose
Smooching party	Kissing
Snatch	Kidnapping
Sneaky Pete	Cheap wine
Sniffing Arizona perfume	Going to the gas chamber
Snort	A drink

"Come on over to Plunkett's and we'll have a snort on it."

> From the novel *Blow Up a Storm*,
> Garson Kanin, 1959

Snow	Cocaine
Snow job	A misleading story, a pack of lies designed to divert attention from the real situation
Snowbird	Cokehead *"My mother sells snow to the snowbirds,* *my father makes barbershop gin,* *my sister sells jazz for a living,* *and that's why the money rolls in."* Jail song from the film *The Young Savages*, 1960
So long, Pal, be pure.	Hipster farewell
So mean you won't even spend a weekend	Stingy, a tightwad
So round, so firm, so fully packed	Good-looking See the country recording "So Round, So Firm, So Fully Packed," Merle Travis, 1947.
Soak your face	Get drunk
Sob sister	Sad, crying, miserable
Sob story	Hard-luck tale, depressing story
Sock	1. Close dancing *" '. . . would you mind, you're dancing too close.'* *Lover grinned. 'Don't like to sock it in, huh?'* *'Why get ourselves all excited?' Mary said,* *looking at him coolly now. 'It's too hot to* *raise a temperature.' "* From the novel *Tomboy*, Hal Ellson, 1952 2. Great, really good, outstanding
Sock hop	Teenage dance party
A sock on the button	A punch in the face

152

Sodom by the Sea	Coney Island
Soft money	Easy money
Solid	Good, in order, righteous

See the jazz recordings "Solid, Jack, Solid," Ollie Shepard, 1938 and also "You're Solid with Me," Lovin' Sam with the Burns Campbell Orchestra, 1938.

"She never ever wants to go to sleep,
she says that everything's solid all-reet . . ."
From the jazz recording "Who Put the Benzedrine in Mrs. Murphy's Ovaltine?" Harry "The Hipster" Gibson, 1946

Solid, Jack, I'll dig you in your den gradually.	The proper reply when invited to someone's house for a visit, according to Cab Calloway's Swingformation Bureau
Solid sender	A real knockout

Down Beat's Yearbook of Swing, 1939, defined a sender as "1. A musician capable of playing good hot solos, and 2. A performance that pleases Swing fans."

"Oh my Linda,
she's a solid sender,
you know you'd better surrender."
From the rock 'n' roll recording "Slippin' and Slidin'," Little Richard, 1956

Roy Milton had an R&B group from 1946 to 1956 called the Solid Senders.

"Boy that man's a solid sender, when he gets riding on that go-toy the cats really start cryin'."
From the film *Orchestra Wives*, 1942

Some dollars to walk and wake up with	Spending money, working capital

Songbird   Female vocalist

> At the Harlem's Lafayette Theatre in July 1919 the
> Five Dixie Girls were being advertised as "A
> Quintette of Classy Songbirds."

Sound   To listen

"Talk up, man, I don't sound you at all . . ."

> From the film *High School Confidential*, 1958

Sounds   Music

Soup   1. High-performance hot-rod fuel, a special
mixture

2. Swearing

*"Kicking him off the team for that little burst
of soup, it wasn't fair. What did the coach have
against him?"*

> From the novel *Scandal High*,
> Herbert O. Pruett, 1960

3. Explosives

*"The two Cs got him. For that many pieces of
paper he could take his chances with a gallon of
soup."*

i.e., *For that much money he'd risk being
blown up.*

> From the novel *Kiss Me, Deadly*,
> Mickey Spillane, 1953

Sourpuss   Bad-tempered, ugly

South of the slot   The wrong side of the tracks, the poor part of
town, from humble beginnings

Southpaw   Left-handed

> See the boogie-woogie recording "Southpaw
> Serenade," Will Bradley and His Orchestra with
> Freddie Slack on piano, 1942.

South view   An interesting viewpoint

*"I am tellin' you that the south view of this dame
from the east when she is walkin' north would make
a blind man turn to hard liquor."*

> From the novel *Your Deal, My Lovely*,
> Peter Cheyney, 1941

Soused	Drunk
	"Poppa's gone up to town. He'll get himself soused and shoot his mouth off."
	From the film *They Live by Night,* 1948
Sousepot	Drunkard
Spare me the hot air.	Shut up, I'm not interested.
Spigot bigot	Prohibitionist, anti-alcohol campaigner
Spill your guts	Confess, tell all, become an informer
	"Little Joe waggled the bottle admonishingly at his companion. 'You hadn't ought to have done that,' he said, 'just when he was going to spill his guts.'"
	From the novel *Headed for a Hearse,* Jonathan Latimer, 1935
Spinach	Dollar bills
Splinter your toupee	Go crazy, flip your wig
Split, no-tomorrow style	Leave in a great hurry
Splitting the freight on a crash pad	Sharing the rent for an apartment
Sporting house	Brothel
Squall and ball and climb the wall	Have a wild time
	This was the catch-phrase of "Smilin' " Eddie Hill, 1940s country performer and DJ on WMC radio in Memphis.
Square a beef	Sort out a problem or a grievance
	"You couldn't square a beef with a stupe."
	i.e., *You can't settle an argument with an idiot.*
	From the novel *The Grifters,* Jim Thompson, 1963

Square from Delaware	Unenlightened person See the jazz recordings "(You're a) Square from Delaware," Fats Waller and His Rhythm, 1940; "It's Square but It Rocks," Count Basie and His Orchestra, 1941; and "Serenade to a Square," Sonny Stitt and The Be Bop Boys, 1946.
Square meal on a round plate	Food
Squawkers	Parents *"Must be a lot of our squawkers could give a finger."* i.e., *A lot of our parents could lend a hand.* From the film *Shake, Rattle and Rock,* 1957
Squeaker	A violinist
Squeaking shoe leather	Walking around
Squeal	Confess
Squealer	Informer
Squirting metal	Firing a gun
Stabbing heels	High heels
Stacked	Well-built, a good figure *"She was stacked. She was pretty. She was just about everything you could want in a woman."* From the novel *Savage Night,* Jim Thompson, 1953
Stacked up	A car crash " 'What happened?' *'I stacked it up,' Brad said slowly, looking her right in the eye. She blinked under his hard, level stare.* *'You,' she said with a gasp. 'You stacked it up? You mean you had an accident?' "* From the novel *Run Tough, Run Hard,* Carson Bingham, 1961

Stagger-juice	Alcohol
	"This dame is plumb full of stagger-juice."
	From the novel *Dames Don't Care*,
	Peter Cheyney, 1937
Stallion	Boyfriend, stud
	"She's been tied in knots with so many stallions, no detective on earth could pick the right goon out of that mob in the restaurant."
	From the novel *Death Is Confidential*,
	Lawrence Lariar, 1959
Stand by while I pad your skull.	Listen carefully.
Stand-up guy	Reliable, helpful, good in a tight spot
	"We'll probably never see each other again after we split up the money and break up tonight, but in my book you'll always be a stand-up guy."
	From the film *The Killing*, 1956
Static	Complaints, noise
	"Hey, that's enough static out of you."
	Station cop to James Dean. From the film *Rebel Without a Cause*, 1955
Stay cool, hang loose, admit nothing	Recommended behavior when dealing with the forces of law and order
Steady as rain	Going steady, having a regular partner
Step-ins	Underwear
Step off	Be executed, killed by the State
Steppin'	Dancing
Steppin' on the gas	Literally, to drive fast, but also just to cut loose and get wild
	See the jazz recording "Steppin' on the Gas," Jimmy O'Bryant's Famous Original Washboard Band, 1925.

Stewed to the gills   Drunk
> The Edison company put out a wax cylinder in 1913 with a comedy sketch called "Funny Doings at Sleepy Hollow," in which one of the characters utters the line "I'm a little stewed, yer see . . ."

Stick   1. Reefer, joint
> See the jazz recording "Burnin' Sticks," Toots Mondello and His Orchestra, 1939.

2. Bar
e.g., *"Behind the stick," where a barman stands.*

Stick with me, you'll come in on the tide.   I'll look after you.
"Stick with us kid, you'll come in on the tide."
> The chorus girls lend Ruby Keeler a hand, from the film *42nd Street,* 1933.

Stiff   Corpse

Stiff one   A drink with a high alcohol content

Stinking   1. Completely drunk
2. Loaded with money

Stir   Prison

Stone   Complete, full

Stone college   Prison

Stoned   1. Drunk
"I would say, roughly, that Dean Martin has been stoned more often than the United States embassies . . ."
> Frank Sinatra onstage at The Sands, Las Vegas, 1966

2. On drugs, particularly marijuana

Stool pigeon   Informer

Storage	Jail
	"*Ah, maybe we better put this nut in storage.*"
	From the novel *Always Leave 'Em Dying*,
	Richard S. Prather, 1961
Stow it.	Shut up.
Stow the hot talk.	Shut up.
Straight dope	The truth, reliable information
	"*Had The Man given me the straight dope? He might have . . .*"
	From the novel *Savage Night*, Jim Thompson, 1953
Straight from the cookhouse	Inside information, a hot tip
Straight from the fridge	Cool
	"*Great dad, great, straight from the fridge.*"
	From the film *Beat Girl*, 1960
Straight, no chaser	The undiluted truth, the real thing, reliable information
	Art Taylor put out a jazz track in 1959 called "Straight, No Chaser."
Straighten up and fly right.	Behave properly, do the decent thing, sort yourself out.
	" '*All right!*' *Schaeffer's voice was savage. He was the cop again.* '*Do what you want. But for God's sake, Pop, come out of it. Straighten up and fly right.*' "
	From the novel *Violent Night*, Whit Harrison, 1952
	"*Straighten up baby,* *Why don't you fly right sometimes,* *That will ease my temperature* *And cool my worried mind.*"
	From the blues recording "Straighten Up Baby," James Cotton, 1954
Stretch	Prison sentence
Strictly for the birds	1. Useless, a pack of lies
	2. It's not for me, I'm not interested
	" '*How do you like being a deputy G-Man, Janson?*'

'It's crazy, man,' I told him. 'Real crazy.
Strictly for the birds.'" i.e., I don't like it.
From the novel *Chicago Chick*, Hank Janson, 1962

Strictly union   Corny music, unadventurous

Stroll   The street

Struggle   Dance
"Hey, how 'bout you? You wanna struggle?"
From the film *The Wild One*, 1954

Struggle buggy   Automobile
See the jazz recording "*Struggle Buggy*," King
Oliver and his Orchestra, 1930.

Strut yo' stuff   Dance, perform, or otherwise show what you're
made of
A theater production called *Strut Yo' Stuff*, billed as
"A Stupendous Musical Satire," was running in
New York in December 1920.

See also the blues recording "Get Yourself a
Monkey Man, and Make Him Strut His Stuff,"
Butterbeans and Susie, 1924.

Struttin'   Dancing
See the blues recordings "I'm a Doggone Struttin'
Fool," Noble Sissle, 1921, and "Learn to Do the
Strut," Don Parker and his Orchestra, 1923.

Stud   Guy, hepcat, dude
"I'm set to drift when Elmo pops up with two other
studs. Elmo's the President of the mob, the boss cat.
He's not too big, but a rough stud when the chips
are down."
From the short story "The Rites of Death,"
Hal Ellson, 1956

Stud dog   Sexually demanding, a bit of a caveman
"She had tried to tell Sylvia that Willie-Joe was a
stud dog."
From the novel *Scandal High*,
Herbert O. Pruett, 1960

Stuff with the dead ones' pictures	Paper money From the autobiography *Really the Blues*, Mezz Mezzrow and Bernard Wolfe, 1946
Suck the bottle	Drink, get drunk *"Four bottles . . . And you sucked up three of 'em. I had to practically clip you to get a swallow. You said your leg hurt 'an you wanted to get drunk."* From the novel *Fast One*, Paul Cain, 1936
Sucker bait	Inducement, advertising
Sucker list	Client base, mailing list
Suds	Beer *" 'I was just thinking,' he said, 'how a nice beer would go right now. A nice, ice-cold suds with about an inch of cuff on it.' "* From the novel *Violent Saturday*, W. L. Heath, 1955
Suitcase	A kit of drums
Suited down	Well-dressed, sharp
Suppose we get together and split a herring?	Would you like to go out with me one night?
Swapping chews	Kissing
Sweating out the rest of it	Serving a life sentence in the slammer
Sweet swingin' sphere	The world *"I'm gonna put a cat on you that's the sweetest, gonest, wailingest cat that ever stomped on this sweet swingin' sphere . . ."* From the spoken word recording *The Nazz*, Lord Buckley, 1951
A swell piece	Good-looking woman
Swelling up like a poisoned pup	Pleased with yourself, conceited, proud

Swing	1. Term for jazz music that became popular from the very end of the 1920s
	Down Beat's Yearbook of Swing, 1939, defined the word as "the latest name for hot jazz music; more freely used as a term applied to all popular jazz."
	See the jazz recording "Swing, You Cats," Louis Armstrong and his Orchestra, 1933.
	2. Mode of behavior
	" *'I don't know,' Frankie sympathized. 'It's just that some cats swing like that, I guess.'* "
	From the novel *The Man with the Golden Arm*, Nelson Algren, 1949
	3. Allegiance
	e.g., *"Which gang do you swing with?"*
Swing shift	Evening work
Swingin'	Cool, crazy, in the groove, the best
Switching channels	Changing your story
Swooner	Someone good-looking
Sympathy	*"Let me put it this way—I should be sincerely sorry to see my neighbor's children devoured by wolves."*
	Waldo Lydecker positively oozing sympathy.
	From the film *Laura*, 1944

T

T.C.B.	Taking care of business—the personal motto of Elvis Presley
Tab-lifter	Nightclub customer
T'aint no crack but a solid fact.	It's the truth.
	From the autobiography *Really the Blues*, Mezz Mezzrow and Bernard Wolfe, 1946

162

Take a bite of air.	Get lost.
Take a raincheck	Pass up an opportunity
Take a run-out powder	Leave in a hurry *"He had too much to lose. Molly would peel him skinless if he ever decided to take a powder."* From the novel *Run Tough, Run Hard*, Carson Bingham, 1961
Take it on the lam	Run from the law
Take off your stomping shoes.	Stop looking for trouble; calm down, I don't want a fight.
Take some hot groceries	Eat a meal
Taken off the payroll	Killed, assassinated
Takes the paint off your deck	It's rough booze, strictly low-class
Talking in dribbles	Speaking rubbish, making no sense
Talking that talk	Speaking in jive-talk, using hipster slang See the vocal group recording "Talk That Talk," The Du Droppers, 1955.
Talking trash	Verbal abuse
Talking turkey	Straight talking, honesty
Tall	Drunk *" 'I think you are a splendid woman,' he said.* *'I'm high, wide and handsome,' she said.* *'I'm tall.'* *'Tall?'* *'High. Tight. Crocked. Drunk.' "* From the novel *Red Gardenias*, Jonathan Latimer, 1939

Tamp on down the stroll	Walk down the street
Tank town	Small town, out in the sticks, the opposite of a big city like New York or Chicago *"What's a fast guy like you doing at a tank-town teacher's college?"* From the novel *Savage Night*, Jim Thompson, 1953
Tanked	Drunk
Tap the bottle	Drink
Tapped	Arrested
Tapping a jug	Robbing a bank *"He blasted a couple of fuzz while he was tapping a jug."* i.e., *He shot a couple of policemen when robbing a bank.* From the novel *Murder on Monday*, Robert Patrick Wilmot, 1952
Tapsville	Broke
Taxi dancer	Paid dancing partner at a dancehall, not the most respectable of professions " *'I can tell you where she works.'* *'Where?'* *'At the Clark-Erie ballroom. She's a hostess there.'* *'A taxi-dancer?'* *'I reckon that's what you calls 'em ...' "* From the novel *The Lady in the Morgue*, Jonathan Latimer, 1936. *"Listen: it's a safe bet Baird's just knocked off one of Rico's taxi-dancers."* From the novel *The Fast Buck*, James Hadley Chase, 1952
Tea	Weed, marijuana *"I didn't know what was happening to me, and I suddenly realized it was only the tea that we were smoking; Dean had bought some in New York. It made me think that everything was about to*

*arrive—the moment when you know all and
everything is decided forever."*
> Sal Paradise grazes on some grass. From the novel
> *On the Road,* Jack Kerouac, 1957

Tea hound — A marijuana smoker

**Tear it down,
soup it up, and
strip it for speed.** — Sort it out, adapt things to suit your own
requirements.

Teenage fluff — Young girl
> From the novel *If He Hollers Let Him Go,*
> Chester Himes, 1945

**Teeth and tongue
will get you hung.** — You talk too much.

Tell it like it is — Straight talking, telling the truth

**Tell that to a
mule and he'll
kick your
head off.** — That's a lie, I don't believe you.

Terpsichorical — Dancing
*"Hey baby, how's about you and me getting
terpsichorical? Let's go downstairs and fly."*
> Oliver Reed invites a charming young lady to
> dance, from the film *Beat Girl,* 1960.

**That ain't second
base.** — Watch where you're going.
*"Man, lookout where you're steppin'.
That ain't second base."*
> From the boogie-woogie recording *"Down the
> Road a Piece,"* Ray McKinley, 1942

**That chick is
locked up in this
direction, so just
cut out while
your conk is all in
one portion.** — "How you can tell someone to stop annoying the
young lady you are escorting."
> From Professor Cab Calloway's
> Swingformation Bureau

That don't move me. I'm not impressed.
> See the rockabilly recording "That Don't Move Me," Carl Perkins, 1956.

That gives me a large charge. I'm excited; I'm impressed.

That thing Sex organs
"My friend picked a new girl
in a little dance-hall
he used to be a high-stepper
but now he can't walk at all
somebody's been using that thing
somebody's been using that thing
just as sure as you're born
somebody's been using that thing."
> From the blues recording "Somebody's Been Using That Thing," The Hokum Boys, 1929

The phrase became something of an obsession with blues songwriters of the twenties and thirties, i.e., "Shake That Thing," Ethel Waters, 1925; "I'm Wild About That Thing," Bessie Smith, 1928; "Let Me Pat That Thing," The Hohum Boys, 1929; "Bury That Thing," Roosevelt Sykes, 1929; "It's a Pretty Little Thing," Tampa Red, 1930; "She's Dangerous with That Thing," Lonnie Johnson, 1931; and, on an educational note, "What's the Name of That Thing?," The Chatman Brothers, 1936.

That vibrates me. I'm impressed; I really like it.

That's a bringer, that's a hanger. That's a bringdown, that's a hang up, that's depressing.
> See the jazz recording "That's a Bringer, That's a Hanger," Slim Gaillard and His Flat Foot Floogie Boys, 1939

That's a gas.
1. That's great; that's really good.
2. That's a laugh; what rubbish.
"Afraid of you? That's a gas! He could stamp you out like an ant. You're nothing to him."
> From the novel *Two Timing Tart,* John Davidson, 1961

166

That's a panic and a half.	That's really amusing.
The words don't go with the music.	I don't believe you.
Them's the breaks, kid.	That's life.
They threw babies out of the balcony.	That performance went down a storm.

They'll pat you with a spade.	You're likely to get yourself killed.
	"I got lead in this here rod and my finger's itching. One crack out of any of you and they'll pat you with a spade."
	    Rico talks tough, from the novel *Little Caesar,*
	    W. R. Burnett, 1929

They're gonna carry you by the handles	Watch your mouth or you'll get yourself killed. *"Keep it up pal, and six of your best friends are gonna be carrying you by the handles . . ."* Dean Martin to heckler, onstage at The Sands, Las Vegas, February 1964
Thin man	Nonexistent person on the payroll, whose wages find their way into the pockets of the boss

Thinking room	Signs of intelligence in the face
	"Her eyes were wide set and there was thinking room between them."
	    From the short story "Trouble Is My Business,"
	    Raymond Chandler, 1939

Thinner than the gold on a weekend wedding ring	Extremely thin
Third degree	Heavy-duty interrogation, often involving fists, clubs, and other subtle methods of persuasion

This bird's gonna pull his freight.	I'm leaving; I'm outta here.
Thou shalt not bug thy neighbor.	The hip commandment i.e., Be cool, don't annoy people.
Threaded down	Well-dressed, sharply turned out
Threads	Clothes
Three sheets to the wind	Drunk
Three singles or a large shakedown?	Three single rooms or a suite?
Three-time loser	Prisoner serving a life sentence after three convictions
Thrill up on the hill	Dance or party *"There's a thrill up on the hill, let's go, let's go, let's go."* From the R&B recording "Let's Go, Let's Go, Let's Go," Hank Ballard, 1960
Throttle jockey	Hot-rodder
Throw that dirt in your face	Being buried *"A guy's got a right to expect his family to show up when the time comes to throw dirt in his face."* From the novel *Halo in Blood,* Howard Browne, 1946 *"I'll hire a black cadillac To drive you to your grave I'm gonna be there baby Throw that dirt in your face I'll wear a black mink coat A diamond ring on my hand Before they put you underground I'll have myself another man . . ."* From the rock 'n' roll recording "Black Cadillac," Joyce Green, 1956

Throwing lead	Shooting, firing guns *"Why, you bone-headed gazooma, you ain't even got a mind o' your own. Okay, so nobody knows him. That's fine. Maybe tomorrow, the day after, some other finger-man'll be up here throwin' lead around. And to think I pay you guys dough. Get the stiff dumped in the river. And for Christ's sake put weights on the feet."* Problems with the hired help, from the novel *Hot Dames on Cold Slabs*, Michael Storme, 1950
Thrush	Female singer
Thumb	Hipster handshake *"Hey Pops, thumb me will ya Daddy-o?"* From the film *The Wild One*, 1954
Tie one on	Get drunk
Tight as a vault with a busted timelock	Closed, impenetrable
Tighten someone's wig	Introduce them to marijuana
Tighteye	Sleep
Tijuana bible	Pornographic magazine
Till-tapper	Thief, store burglar
Tin ears strictly around the block	Unsophisticated people From the film *High School Confidential*, 1958
Tip-top daddy	Suave, in the groove, a righteous dude
Tip your hole card	Give the game away, reveal your intentions
Tip your mitt	See "tip your hole card."
Toeology	Tapdancing

e.g., *"An upstate guy wigs you with some most burnt toeology."*
i.e., *A hip dude impresses you with the skill of his tapdancing.*

Togged to the bricks   Dressed up, sharply turned out, suave

Tomato   Good-looking woman
"Here was I in my own apartment with three beautiful tomatoes and all I could think of was getting rid of them. Life can be really cruel sometimes."
> From the short story "The Live Ones," Richard S. Prather, 1956

"She's a real sad tomato, She's a busted valentine . . ."
> Lauren Bacall's song from *The Big Sleep,* 1946

"Give a lift to a tomato, you expect her to be nice, don't you?"
> From the film *Detour,* 1945

Tonsil paint   Alcohol

Too lovely to feed to the hogs   Very attractive, good-looking

Toots   1. Term of affection,
e.g., *"Best take a shot, toots."*
i.e., *Have a drink, honey.*

Sometimes the word is spelled "tutz," as in "How're you gettin' along with tutz?"
> From the novel *Red Gardenias,* Jonathan Latimer, 1939

2. Patronizing or threatening term of address
" 'Watch your step, Toots,' he said evenly. 'I shan't tell you again.' "
> From the novel *The Fast Buck,* James Hadley Chase, 1952

Top eliminator	The fastest hot-rod, or hot-rod driver, total shutdown artist
Top storey	Head, brain
Top stud	The leader, the head honcho, the boss
Too much	The best, really good, a total knockout See the vocal group recording "Much Too Much," The Hollywood Flames, 1959.
Torn up	Wasted, upset, ragged, unsettled, maybe impressed
Torpedo	Gunman, hit man
Torso-tosser	Hoochie-coochie dancer, strip artist
Tough enough to swap punches with a power shovel	Hard, resilient, not exactly a pushover
Tramp on it.	Hurry up; get moving; go faster. *"Tramp on it, friend, make speed."* From the novel *The Little Sister*, Raymond Chandler, 1949
Trash	Gossip, chatter, loose talk
Trifling	Unfaithful *"Who's been playin' around with you,* *a real cool cat with eyes of blue?* *Trifling baby are you being true,* *who's been fooling around with you?"* From the rockabilly recording "Red Cadillac and Black Mustache," Warren Smith, 1957
Triggerman	Assassin, hit man *"He'd killed several men. Nobody knew how many except George, and he probably couldn't count that high. He'd been a trigger-man for a couple of the top*

men of the U.S. crime syndicate, and was noted for his efficiency and stupidity."

> From the novel *Darling, It's Death,*
> Richard S. Prather, 1953

Trottery Dancehall

Troubled with the shorts Broke, poverty-stricken

> From the autobiography *Really the Blues,*
> Mezz Mezzrow and Bernard Wolfe, 1946

Trucking 1. Fucking

> See the blues recordings "Let's Get Drunk and Truck," The Harlem Hamfats, 1936; "Caught My Gal Truckin'," Tampa Red, 1936; and the country recording "Can't Nobody Truck Like Me," Cliff Bruner's Texas Wanderers, 1937.

2. A dance made popular at the Cotton Club in Harlem in the early 1930s

" 'Aw, come on, Camelia,' called Miss Day, moving her torso slowly from side to side. 'I'd like to do a little truckin'.' "

> From the novel *The Dead Don't Care,*
> Jonathan Latimer, 1937

3. Walking

"*Truck on down and dig me, Jack . . .*"

> From the R&B jump jive recording
> "Five Guys Named Moe," Louis Jordan &
> The Tympany Five, 1942

Trust One of the great virtues

"*I trusted Amy about as far as I could have pushed the tractor and trailer with two broken legs.*"

> From the novel *The Lady Is a Lush,*
> Orrie Hitt, 1960

Tuckered out Worn out, exhausted

Tucson blanket A newspaper, the usual item of hobo bedding, also known as a California blanket

Turn on the phonograph Confess to the police

Turn the duke	Shortchange someone
Turning your damper down	Sexually satisfied See the country recording "I Think I'll Turn Your Damper Down," Jimmie Davis, 1937
	"With a blonde-headed woman you need to get around, but a black-haired girl will turn your damper down." From the rockabilly recording "Forty-nine Women," Jerry Irby and The Texas Ranchers, 1956
Twicin'	1. Cheating on your partner, sleeping with two people at once 2. Doublecrossing
Twist	Woman, dame, doll *"The twist might die . . . there was a prowl car not more than ten yards away. I had to hit her."* Yet another James Hadley Chase character comes over all chivalrous and sensitive. From the novel *The Fast Buck,* 1952
Two-bit porch climber	Low-class house burglar
Two hands full of piano	A damn good player, hot stuff at whippin' that ivory *"He had the beat to steady down a little combination, just like a good drummer. He really kept two hands full of piano."* From the novel *Blues for the Prince,* Bart Spicer, 1950
Typewriter	Machine gun

U

Ufftay	Tough
Ultimate yelp	Superlative, the best

"She is the last word—the ultimate yelp."
From the novel *Your Deal My Lovely*,
Peter Cheyney, 1941

Under glass In prison

Underpinning Legs

Undertaker's friend Gun, firearm

Unglued Worked up, losing it, flipping your wig
Elvis kisses his co-star, then asks: "How's your headache?," to which she replies, "I'm coming all unglued . . ."
From the film *Jailhouse Rock*, 1957

Unhook your ears, Dad Listen closely
From the film *Shake, Rattle and Rock*, 1957

Unwound Losing it, falling to pieces, cracking up

Up jumped the devil An unexpected piece of bad fortune
"Then up jumped the devil, like the crap-shooters say when seven pops up wrong."
From the autobiography *Rap Sheet*,
Blackie Audett, 1955

Up north In jail
"Pimping will get you a couple of years up north."
From the novel *The Drowning Pool*,
Ross MacDonald, 1950

Upping some real crazy riffs Playing cool music

Uptight 1. Worried, tense
2. In trouble

Used-to-be Ex-lover
See the blues recording "I'm Going Back to My 'Used to Be'," Bessie Smith & Clara Smith, 1924.

"You say you're through with me,
You're settin' me free,
You're just out with your used-to-be . . ."
> From the rockabilly recording "I Can't Hardly
> Stand It," Charlie Feathers, 1956

V

Vag	Vagrant, hobo, bum

"Look at you, all bunged-up like a barrel-house
vag . . ."
> The police captain takes a dim view of the battered
> appearance of one of his detectives.

> From the film *Where the Sidewalk Ends,* 1950

Vamoose	Run away, leave in a hurry, get lost
Varicose alley	Strip club runway
Vines	Suits, jackets, hipster threads

> Babs Gonzales tells the story in his 1967
> autobiography, *I, Paid My Dues,* of how Charlie
> Parker apologized for stealing some of his suits:
> "Babs, baby, I know I downed your vines, so here's
> the tickets." i.e., I stole your clothes, and
> here are the pawnshop tickets.

Viper	Marijuana smoker

> See the jazz recordings "The Viper's Drag,"
> Cab Calloway and His Orchestra, 1930;
> "Song of the Vipers," Louis Armstrong and
> His Orchestra, 1934; and "Sendin' the Vipers,"
> Mezz Mezzrow Orchestra, 1934.

Vomit on the table	Speak up; let's hear what you've got to say.

"Come on, fess up. Vomit on the table . . ."
> From the novel *Go, Man, Go!,*
> Edward De Roo, 1959

Voodoo boilers	A kit of drums

W

Waffle iron	The electric chair
Wail	Cut loose, let off steam, have a wild time

"Now, if you're gonna stay cool, you've got to wail, you've got to put something down, you've got to make some jive. Do you know what I'm saying?"
> Marlon Brando tells it like it is. From the film
> *The Wild One*, 1954

Walking papers	Release from jail
Walking spanish	Being frog-marched out of somewhere
Wanna oil your ankles?	Would you care to dance?
Want a real rear?	Do you want something that'll really get you high?

" 'Want a real rear?' she inquired.
'Laudanum?'
'Yeah. A dash with the next whisky.' "
> From the novel *Red Gardenias*,
> Jonathan Latimer, 1939

Want a weed?	Would you like a cigarette?
Warble	Sing

"They do tell me lots of dames make the grade if they can warble a few notes and if they can show a shapely pair o' gams."
> From the novel *Hot Dames on Cold Slabs*,
> Michael Storme, 1950

Phonograph Monthly Review *from New York ran a "Miscellaneous Warblers" column in its dance music reviews section in the early 1930s.*

Watch my smoke.	I'm outta here; I'm gone.

Ways like a mowing machine	Agricultural metaphor for good sexual technique
	"She's long, she's tall,
	She's a handsome queen,
	She's got ways like a mowing machine."
	    From the country recording "She's a Hum
	    Dum Dinger," Buddy Jones, 1941
	
	Compare this to the blues recording "I've Got Ford
	Movements in My Hips," Cleo Gibson and Her Hot
	Three, 1929.

Wax a disc	To make a recording
Wear the green	Have some paper money
Wearing a concrete footmuff	Taking a swim in the river with your feet encased in concrete, courtesy of the Mafia

Wearing lead buttons on your vest	Getting shot
	" 'Talk like that to me,' Morny said, 'and you are
	liable to be wearing lead buttons on your vest.' "
	    From the novel *The High Window,*
	    Raymond Chandler, 1943

Weedhead	Cannabis smoker
	    See the blues recording "Weedhead Woman,"
	    Champion Jack Dupree, 1939.

Week at the knees	Unsuccessful courtship e.g., *"Man, I spent a week at the knees once, never* *got any further."*

Weiner or Wiener	Penis
	    In Nelson Algren's 1941 novel *Never Come*
	    Morning, the prostitute Tooki asks a prospective
	    client, "Ain't you gonna play Hide the Weenie,
	    Hon? C'mon, Slim, let's slam it around a little."
	
	"Some said it takes hot water
	Baby can't you see,
	But your heat baby

Is plenty warm enough for me,
Baby please warm my weiner . . ."
"Please Warm My Weiner," Bo Carter
(Bo Chatman), 1936

Wet your tonsils	Drink
What do you shake them for?	How do you earn a living? What's your occupation?
What do you think of the stackup?	How does the situation appear to you?

What know, man?	Hipster form of greeting
	    From the autobiography *I, Paid My Dues*,
	    Babs Gonzales, 1967

What's all the shooting about?	What's up? Why the fuss? From the film *Don't Knock the Rock*, 1956
What's on the agenda, Brenda?	What's happening? How are you doing?

What's the belch, friend?	What's happening? What's the news?
	    From the novel *Halo in Blood*,
	    Howard Browne, 1946

What's cookin'? Nothin' but spaghetti, and it ain't ready.	Nothing's happening, I don't have any news.

What's the good word?	What's happening? What's the news?
	    Used by Dashiell Hammett in the novel
	    The Glass Key, 1931

What's the pitch?	What's the story? What's happening?
What's tickin', chicken?	What's happening? How are you?

Wheel a spiel	Make a speech, talk big
When they made you, they scraped off the mould.	You're a louse, you're the lowest of the low.
Where do you hang hat?	Where are you from? Where are you staying?
Whippin' that ivory	Playing the piano
A whiskey sour to all the beer in Brooklyn	A dead certainty, a sure thing
Whisper	Rumor, news
Whistle bait	A good-looking woman, someone worth whistling at *"Her name was Rhoda Stern. She didn't have to tell us that she wasn't whistle bait, if she ever had been."* From the novel *The Lenient Beast*, Fredric Brown, 1957
Whistling through the graveyard	Bluffing, putting up a front *"Phil Duncan slid two blue chips into the center of the table. 'Two blues say you're whistling through the graveyard.' "* From the novel *This Is Murder*, Erle Stanley Gardner, 1935
Who broke your doll?	Why are you crying? *" 'What's the pitch, bitch?' I demanded. 'Who broke your doll?' "* Matt Helm comes over all sensitive and concerned, from the novel *Murderer's Row*, Donald Hamilton, 1961.
Wholesale banking business	Bank robbery

Whoopee   Mostly this was a euphemism for sex, although it was also taken more generally to mean having a good time, whooping it up.

"Most always when a man leaves his wife, there's no excuse in the world for him. She may have been making whoop-whoop-whoopee with the whole ten commandments, but if he shows his disapproval to the extent of walking out on her, he will thereafter be a total stranger to all his friends."
   From the short story "Ex Parte,"
   Ring Lardner, 1920s

"Lonnie Johnson goes in for the fantastically macabre in his blues "She's Making Whoopee in Hell Tonight" and "Death Valley Is Half Way to My Home."
   From the magazine *Phonograph Monthly Review*,
   New York, April 1930

*"I was out last night
At the cabaret,
Came in this morning
'Bout the break of day
Been makin' whoopee . . ."*
   From the blues recording "Tight Whoopee,"
   Mozelle Alderson, 1930

   See the jazz song "Makin' Whoopee," written
   by Walter Donaldson in 1928, for the
   Broadway show *Whoopee!*

Whoopee mama   Good-time girl, flapper, party animal

Why did you do me this way?   How could you treat me like that?

Wide-open town   Wild, lawless, packed with late-night entertainment
"Aw, come on, man. Have a couple of drinks and you'll feel better. This is a wide-open town."
   From the novel *The Drowning Pool*,
   Ross MacDonald, 1950

Wig	1. Head or hair See the jazz recording "Gassin' the Wig," Roy Porter, 1948. 2. Mind
Wig chop	A haircut
Wig out	Go crazy, have a wild time, enjoy
Wig tightener	Something, or someone, very impressive
Wiggle	Dance, strut your stuff *"She's got a wiggle* *Make a dead man awake,* *She don't rock* *She just stands there and shakes."* From the rockabilly recording "My Baby Don't Rock," Luke McDaniel, 1957
Windy	Scared, apprehensive
Wine Spo-Dee-O-Dee	An obscene U.S. Army drinking song The lyrics were cleaned up slightly by Stick McGhee for his 1949 R&B recording entitled "Drinking Wine Spo-Dee-O-Dee." The original lyric went "Drinking wine, mother-fucker, drinking wine . . ." By the time Jack Kerouac got around to including the term in his novel *On the Road* (1957), it had somehow become just another name for a drink: "Dean and I had ended up with a colored guy called Walter who ordered drinks at the bar and had them lined up and said 'Wine-spodiodi!' which was a shot of port wine, a shot of whisky, and a shot of port wine. 'Nice sweet jacket for all that bad whisky!' he yelled."
Wino time	A short jail sentence
Wiper	Assassin, hit man, rub-out artist

Wise guy	1. Mobbed up, a made man, a member of the Mafia
	2. Smart aleck
	" 'A wise guy!' Bert commented, slapping me across the face . . ."
	    From the novel *Two Timing Tart*,
	    John Davidson, 1961

Wise up	1. Get smart 2. To educate or inform someone
Woo number	Girlfriend or boyfriend
Wooden kimono	Coffin
Woodpile	Xylophone
Woodshed	*"A place for a private rehearsal, often used as a verb, meaning to practice in private."* From *Down Beat's Yearbook of Swing*, 1939

Wordsville	A library
	"Look out, or we'll be thrown out of Wordsville."
	    From the novel *Run Tough, Run Hard*,
	    Carson Bingham, 1961

Working for the Woolworths	Doing a low-paid job, i.e., for nickels and dimes
Working your groundsmashers overtime	1. Moving fast 2. Dancing in an impressive fashion

Wouldst like to con a glimmer early with me this black?	Would you like to go to a movie with me this evening?
	    From Professor Cab Calloway's
	    Swingformation Bureau

Wound up like an eight-day clock	Uptight, tense, stressed out

Wrecking crew	Police interrogation operatives
	"Take this baby down the cellar and let the wrecking crew work on him before you lock him up."
	From the novel *Red Harvest*, Dashiell Hammett, 1929

The Wrecking Crew was the title of a novel from 1960 which was part of Donald Hamilton's Matt Helm series, the film versions of which starred Dean Martin, and it was also the collective name for the regular musicians who played on Phil Spector's Wall of Sound recordings in the early sixties.

A wrong gee	A bad sort, an untrustworthy guy
Wrong side of the tracks	The bad part of town, low-down, poverty row

---

X-ray eyes	*"Either we got X-ray eyes, or those babies are dancing in their underwear."*
	The lure of the taxi-dancehall becomes apparent to a first-time customer. From the novel *The Lady in the Morgue*, Jonathan Latimer, 1936

Yak	Talk
	"If there's anything I can't stand, it's a cheap jerk who yakkity-yaks all the time. Kick him in the teeth if he keeps talking, Pete."
	From the novel *The Deadly Lover*, Robert O. Saber, 1951
	"I was so stunned I let him keep on yakking."
	From the novel *Always Leave 'Em Dying*, Richard S. Prather, 1961

Yaks   Laughs, fun
"*We had a lotta yaks, huh Johnny?*"
From the film *The Wild One*, 1954

Yammer   Talk

Yap   1. Talk
2. Mouth
e.g., "*Shut your yap.*"

Yard   One hundred dollars
After 1930 it often meant one thousand dollars.

Yas Yas Yas   Ass, backside
"*I used to play slow but now I play it fast,
just to see the women shake their yas, yas, yas . . .*"
From the blues recording "Shack Bully Stomp,"
Peetie Wheatstraw, 1938

See also the blues recordings "The Duck's Yas Yas
Yas," James Stump Johnson & Alex Hill, 1929
and "Yas Yas Yas Number 1," Jimmy Strange
(The Yas Yas Man), 1936.

Yegg   1. Criminal. Originally this was a specific term
for a safe-cracker, but came to have a more
general use
"*The big man was a yegg. San Fransisco was on fire
for him.*" i.e., *He was a criminal, and he was the
object of a city-wide manhunt.*
From the short story "Fly Paper,"
Dashiell Hammett, 1920s

"*The dame shrugged her bare shoulders. 'You know
it all, mac. Sure, my old man was a gangster, a
tough yegg . . .'*"
From the novel *The Corrupt Ones*,
J. C. Barton, circa 1950
2. A beggar

**You ain't just
whistling Dixie.**   That's right, I agree with you;
you're speaking the truth.

You are a triple scream and one big yell. I really like you.

You burn me up.
1. You excite me.
2. You make me angry.
   See the jazz recording "Cold Mamas Burn Me Up," Bailey's Lucky Seven, 1924.

You can cook him up brown. You can get your own back; you can have your revenge.
"If you want to get back at him, here's your chance. You can cook him up brown."
   From the novel *Violent Night*,
   Whit Harrison, 1952

You can sing two choruses of that. You can say that again.

You can take that to the bank and cash it. It's the truth; I mean it; this is reliable information.

You fracture me. You make me laugh.
" *'You fracture me, Elmer,' she said. 'To look at you, a person would think you just came in with a car-load of cattle.'* "
   From the novel *Little Men, Big World*,
   W. R. Burnett, 1951

You give me hot pants. I find you very attractive.

You got any happy money on you? It'll cost you.
" *'You got any happy money on you?'*
'Happy money?'
'Yeah. Money that's gonna make me happy, what else?'
'How much?'
'Fifty dollars.' "
   From the film *Pickup on South Street*, 1953

You jet me.	You're the most; I'm really impressed. *"You positively jet me! Gone, gone, gone!* *Jet, jet, jet!"* From the novel *Go, Man, Go!*, Edward De Roo, 1959
You paralyze me.	You make me laugh; you surprise me; you knock me out.
You said a mouthful.	That's the truth; that's it exactly.
You send me.	I'm gone; you flip me out; I'm impressed. See the ballad "You Send Me," Sam Cooke, 1957. *"Every time she loves me* *She sends my mellow soul."* From the boogie-woogie recording "Roll 'Em, Pete," Pete Johnson and Joe Turner, 1938
You send me to the end.	You *really* send me.
You snap the whip, I'll make the trip.	I'll do what you say, I'm all yours.
You'd better get your flaps down or you'll take off.	Don't get so excited, calm down. From the first film version of *Farewell, My Lovely*, 1944
You'll find my name on the tail of my shirt.	Traditional response to police questioning, especially by tramps and drifters *"Told them my name was on the tail of my shirt,* *I'm a Tennessee hustler, I don't have to work . . ."* From the country recording "T for Texas (Blue Yodel No. 1)," Jimmie Rodgers, 1927
Your brain's a little dusty.	You're rather stupid; you're not thinking straight.
Your roof is leaking.	You're not all there; you're a little crazy.

Your teeth are swimming.	You're plastered; you're full up with booze. *"You're drunk, Al. Your teeth are swimming."* From the novel *What Makes Sammy Run?*, Budd Schulberg, 1941
You're a panic.	You crack me up; you're really funny.
You're killing me with your sad pan.	Why the long face? You look depressed.
You're my habit, rabbit.	I dig you the most.
You're not comin' through at all.	You're making no sense, explain yourself.
You're not just saying it.	That's right, I agree with you.
You're stepping on your motor to hear your cut-out roar.	You're bragging; you're all talk.
You're talking on a dead phone.	I'm not interested; save your breath.
You're the swinging end.	You're the best.
You've got a crust.	You've got nerve. *"You've got a hell of a crust assuming I'll go down there and take a getaway stake to somebody I know the police are looking for."* From the novel *The Lady in the Lake*, Raymond Chandler, 1944 *" 'To hell with you,' she blazed. 'You got a crust, tearing my clothes like that.' "* From the novel *Homicide Lost*, William Vance, 1956

You've got a date with the fireless cooker.	They're going to send you to the electric chair.
You've got my nose wide open.	You've got me all worked up. " 'You'd better take it easy from now.' 'That's what I intend to do, only trouble is m'nose opens up and I can't tell what I'm doing.' " From the novel *On the Road,* Jack Kerouac, 1957 See the R&B recording *"When It Rains It Really Pours,"* Billy The Kid Emerson, 1955. Also the vocal group recording *"She's Got His Nose Wide Open,"* Ike Perry and The Lyrics, 1960.
You've had your chance and folded.	You wasted the opportunity; you blew it.

Z

Zip gun	Home made pistol, Saturday night special
Zip your lip.	Keep quiet.
Zoot suit	Draped and sculpted hepcat suit. Long in the body, narrow at the waist, as worn by his Royal Hepness, Cab Calloway, onstage at Harlem's Cotton Club. Very popular with the Chicano gangs in Los Angeles during the early stages of World War II, memorably described by James Ellroy in his novel *The Black Dahlia* as "Reet-pleat, drape-shape, stuff-cuff, Argentinian-ducktailed Mexican gangsters." This type of clothing was condemned by Government officials as a waste of cloth and counter-productive to the war effort. A particularly brutal series of gang rumbles which broke out in 1943 were known in the press as the Zoot Suit Wars.

"The young hoodlums wore long coats, pegged pants and drooping keychains. They were about eighteen. They looked out at the world coldly and arrogantly. A tough place, chum! But we're tougher."
From the novel *Little Men, Big World,*
W. R. Burnett, 1951

See the jazz recording "A Zoot Suit (for My Sunday Gal)," Bob Crosby and His Orchestra, 1942.

Permissions

A good-faith effort has been made to secure the permissions to reprint all of the excerpts in this book. In a small number of instances, I have been unable to locate the copyright holder despite my efforts. In such instances the copyright holders are welcome to contact me through the publisher, and we will be glad to include the proper copyright information in all future editions of the book.

Max Décharné

started out as the Gallon Drunk drummer before graduating to lead singer of the Flaming Stars. He is also an author and journalist for *Mojo* and *Bizarre*. He currently divides his time between London and Berlin.